INTERIBERICA, S.A. DE EDICIONES

EARTH IN DANGER
Pollution and Conservation

Doubleday and Company Inc.,
Garden City, New York, 1977
A Windfall Book

© 1976 Interiberica, S. A. - Madrid
© 1976 Aldus Books Limited, London
SBN: 385–11345–5
Library of Congress Catalog Card No: 75–13112

Also published in parts as Pollution and
Conservation

EARTH IN DANGER

Part 1
Pollution

by Ian Breach

ISBN: 84-382-0019-2. Dep. Legal: M. 1369-1976.

Printed and bound in Spain by Novograph
S.A., and Roner S.A., Crta de Irun, Km.12,450,
Madrid–34

Series Coordinator	Geoffrey Rogers
Series Art Director	Frank Fry
Design Consultant	Guenther Radtke
Editorial Consultant	Donald Berwick
Series Consultant	Malcolm Ross-Macdonald
Art Editor	Douglas Sneddon
Editor	Damian Grint
Copy Editor	Maureen Cartwright
Research	Barbara Fraser
Art Assistant	Michael Turner

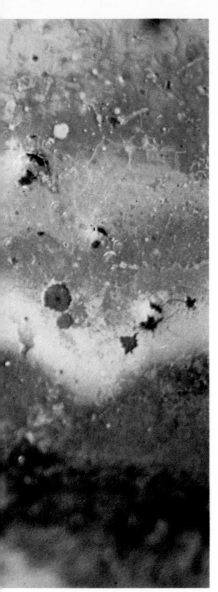

Contents: Part 1

Editoral Advisers

DAVID ATTENBOROUGH Naturalist and Broadcaster

MICHAEL BOORER, B.SC. Author, Lecturer, and Broadcaster

Foreword by David Attenborough

Earth in Danger *is a book crucially different from the others in this series. They describe the natural world largely as it was before man began to dominate it. They show jungles, deserts, mountains, and seas, inhabited by a multitude of animals and plants all miraculously matched to their place in the environment, the result of thousands, in many cases millions, of years of gradual evolutionary change. But over the last hundred years, with terrifying acceleration, many environments have changed beyond recognition. Forests have been replaced by deserts. Streams full of fish, busy with insects and thick with plants have been turned into fetid sewers. And where once immense herds of wild creatures grazed, there are now only sad remnants, greatly reduced not only in numbers but in the variety of species. The cause of this globe-wide change is mankind—ourselves.*

With devastating clarity Ian Breach shows what we have done, partly from greed, partly from thoughtlessness, but largely from ignorance. Previous generations could perhaps claim with some justice that they simply did not foresee the consequences of their actions, or imagine that a simple failure to deal properly with the waste from their factories and towns could lead to such despoilation. But no such excuses can be claimed by us. The crimes of pollution and their consequences are plain for all to see in these pages. Michael Crawford, in the second half of the book, has a slightly happier story to tell. At least he can write of men and organizations working devotedly to try and stem disaster. But the problems of conservation are gigantic and they are only just beginning to be tackled.

Because the book is concerned with the action of men, and because it urges us to change our ways, it is, in the widest sense of the word, political. Politics is not a science. So the chapters that follow necessarily contain the personal views of the authors, passionately held and strongly argued. If I may add one of my own, and one that they touch on only fleetingly, it is that the root-cause of our ecological problems is overpopulation. Over the past few centuries, the number of human beings in the world has increased astronomically. Whereas at one time men could easily find space for their homes and had no difficulties in finding all the raw materials they needed, today we have overrun the earth and carelessly devastated vast areas of its surface denuding it of valuable resources to meet our short-term purposes. Whereas once the effluents from our homes and factories were easily swept away by tides and winds to be recycled by nature, now there are so many of us that the seas and the sky are not big enough to cope with the overwhelming quantities of waste and we are choking in our own filth. The yearly increase in population shows no sign of slackening, but it cannot continue indefinitely without ending in disaster. And that is why the questions raised in this book must be tackled and answered, ultimately not just by biologists or people with a special interest in natural history, but by politicians. And therefore, by us all.

David Attenborough.

The Meaning of Pollution

Pollution is a controversial subject. It is by no means easy to agree on what constitutes pollution, for different people in different circumstances see the problem from widely differing vantage points. Shifting social standards play a large part in determining what seems to be environmentally unacceptable. Thus, when coal and labor were cheaply available to industry, smoking chimneys were universally welcomed as signs of plentiful employment and prosperity. Even for many years after the inhuman conditions and squalid environments of mid-19th-century industrial areas had been largely rooted out, a pall of black factory smoke and a river choked with industrial effluent signalized economic good times to people. It is only recently that we have stopped being blind to the potentially disastrous effects of such things.

Even today, attitudes have not changed as much as one might imagine. In my native county of Lancashire, England—the cradle of the 18th-century Industrial Revolution—working people used to say, "Wheer there's muck there's brass" (in other words, filth and money are inseparable). Variations on that philosophy can still be heard. In recent discussions with a number of people who are actively concerned with the problems of industrial pollution, I have found almost nobody who does not agree that those problems are virtually insoluble in the industrialized nations (mainly in North America, Europe, and Japan). *Some* pollution, they say, must accompany industrial activities; it should be regarded as one of the prices that must be paid for growth and a high standard of living.

One trouble with this view is that it disregards the entire question of who will *ultimately* pay the environmental penalties of our industrial production. We cannot even guess at the extent of those penalties, for we are far from fully understanding the world's natural systems. There are, quite literally, countless examples in the last few

This painting, Industrial Landscape *(by L. S. Lowry), vividly sums up the polluted environment of a factory town in the North of England 40 years ago. Such scenes are still familiar in all parts of the industrialized world.*

Scrapped steam locomotives, rusting away in a railway graveyard, illustrate a typical paradox. Steam engines used to fill the air with soot and smoke; their electric replacements are much cleaner—but the manufacture of modern equipment produces additional pollution and the air is now contaminated at electricity-generating stations.

decades of human intervention in natural processes, where we have pushed dangerously beyond our comprehension of the world's delicate environmental links. To understand how and why we have come to dare too much, let us begin by taking a brief look at past history.

Throughout the centuries, man has evolved a conqueror's attitude toward his natural surroundings. Determined to take more from nature than it was prepared to yield untouched, he has shaped those surroundings for his own betterment. The changes he has made have been colossal in scale, and many of his mistaken attempts to exploit the environment have been resisted, thwarted, or rewarded with catastrophe. But during the scores of centuries between the dawn of civilization and modern times, the disasters were always local and temporary.

By degrees, man learned just how much he could impose his will on nature without suffering a backlash. He discovered how to farm without damaging the soil and how to dam water reserves without causing landslides. He learned to compromise with the forces of nature in order to secure his own well-being.

The instinct for self-preservation seems to be strongest where human beings live and work in small communities. Until after the mid-18th century, human settlements tended to be small and scattered. In 1750 there were fewer than 700 million people alive on this earth, as compared with today's 4000 million, and big cities were rare. In the 18th century, for instance, only one third of Britain's 7 million inhabitants lived in a large town. Today, nearly nine tenths of the 55 million British people live in urban concentrations of more than 100,000. Of the world's entire population, almost half live in cities.

The consequences of rapid population growth and urban concentration have been profound. The 18th-century country-dweller thought little about economic growth; he assumed that his children would be provided for as comfortably or as frugally as he himself was, and by much the same means: farming or some type of craft. That has all changed. Since the beginning of the Industrial Revolution, fewer and fewer people have been engaged in production, and at the same time an increasing and increasingly demanding number have become consumers.

Population growth was at first much faster in the newly industrialized countries than in the rest of the world, and manufacturers strove to sell to vastly enlarged home markets. Thus was established a pattern of industrial and urban development that still remains essentially unchanged. It soon became physically difficult for people to see or feel the natural environment on which they still depended. The pressures of a person's life tended to sap the concern he might have shown for his environment; he was too busy—or too poor—to worry about anything more than his own material well-being.

Life, generally, *did* get better in time. It would be wrong to pretend that the infested cities and rural slums of the pre-industrial Western world represent "the good old days." Indeed, by the middle of the 19th century, advances in agriculture, industry, transportation, and medicine had immensely improved the lot of many Western families. But environmental distress nonetheless existed on a large scale in the smoke-filled, filthy cities. After about 1830, there were frequent epidemics of cholera and typhoid, and, as one writer tells us, "an appalling constant toll of the two great groups of 19th-century urban killers—air

Industrial growth has led to a colossal increase in population and to even more crowded cities, with consequent waste-disposal and environmental problems. This sports-stadium crowd is a mere sampling of the 4000 million people now on earth.

pollution and water pollution, or respiratory and intestinal disease."

And yet the cities continued to grow. In some cities of the West, there has been an apparent reversal in this trend since the 1950s. But the movement of the wealthy to residential suburbs or dormitory commuter districts has simply enlarged the cities and left the inner areas in a worse plight than ever, with spreading slums, increasing sanitation problems, and fewer inhabitants who have the resources to do something about them. Meanwhile, the demand for more and more food and manufactured goods in the cities compels not only industry but also agricultural interests to make their own extraordinary demands upon nature's limited re-sources—and, worse, to tamper with nature in ways undreamed of in earlier centuries. This is particularly true of the developing countries. The catastrophes that resulted from man's exploitation of the environment in the past were as nothing compared with what probably lies ahead.

By the 1960s, there was a growing public awareness of pollution as a grave and universal problem. In America, much of the early credit for this belongs to Rachel Carson's famous book *Silent Spring*, which alerted millions of people to the dangers of indiscriminate crop treatment by pesticides. Although some of her assertions were poorly founded and her critics (many of them from the agricultural chemical industries) quick to point out the flaws, the alarms she rang were

Oil, rubber, metal, plastic: this once beautiful beach on the French coast is littered with bits of the world's trash, some dumped locally, the rest brought in on the tides. In parts of the Mediterranean, bathing is now forbidden because of the health risk caused by pollution.

taken seriously at both official and popular levels. Three years after her book was published, President John Kennedy's Science Advisory Committee concluded simply that "elimination of the use of pesticides should be the goal." Miss Carson's work, which had taken the better part of 15 years to complete, eventually led to the setting up of the U.S. Environmental Protection Agency.

Meanwhile, public concern both in America and abroad was kept alive as a growing number of scientists and public figures asked questions about the environmental side effects of many branches of modern technology. Sir Francis Chichester, the renowned lone sailor, discovered — and publicized the depressing fact — that solid waste was in evidence all over the world's oceans; he claimed that not a single stretch of sea, however remote, was free of garbage. Thor Heyerdahl reported oil pollution on 43 out of 57 days of a mid-ocean voyage. Such comments hardly surprised informed observers of the environmental scene. They knew that a large proportion of

industrial waste reaches the sea, and that much of it is insoluble and will float on for years.

A number of dramatic "accidents" helped to arouse public concern. Major spills from tankers and offshore wells caused authorities their worst headaches, for beaches were fouled with black crude oil, and thousands of birds were killed or cruelly drenched in it. But few people took much notice of such undramatic evidence of pollution as the slow build-up of thin films of oil on the ocean surface, which is essentially a much greater long-term ecological threat than a large but localized oil slick. By the mid-1970s, as many as 10 or 12 million tons of oil annually were being added to the world's waters through accident, carelessness, or sheer irresponsibility. The extent and character of the resultant damage to living resources is as yet incalculable.

The campaigns against pollution that were mounted during the 1960s and early 1970s were at one and the same time valuable *and* misleading. The massive discharge of poisonous phosphates into America's rivers and lakes so upset people—laymen, ecologists, anglers, and others—that there was a general attempt to replace phosphate-based detergents by less toxic and more biodegradable materials. This was a commendable effort; but when another detergent material—nitrilo-triacetic acid (NTA)—was suggested as an acceptable alternative, environmentalists moved too hastily to support the suggestion. Who was to say that NTA *was* a suitable alternative? They had not researched it and could therefore not be sure; "solutions" of this kind have to be monitored very carefully (and at great cost), to ensure that they do not create more, and sometimes more serious, problems than those they hope to solve.

Campaigners and protesters have too often missed the real point and have recommended cures for the disease rather than prevention. The campaign for recycling waste paper is a good example. Environmental groups that argue for the reuse of paper products often fail to consider the energy costs of the recycling process. And proponents of recycling may also ignore the fact that merely reusing waste paper does not prevent industrial growth. Indeed, it may encourage the manufacture of more paper, which could mean an increase in pollution levels and the disappearance of still more trees. Would it not be more satisfactory to strive for a drastic reduction in

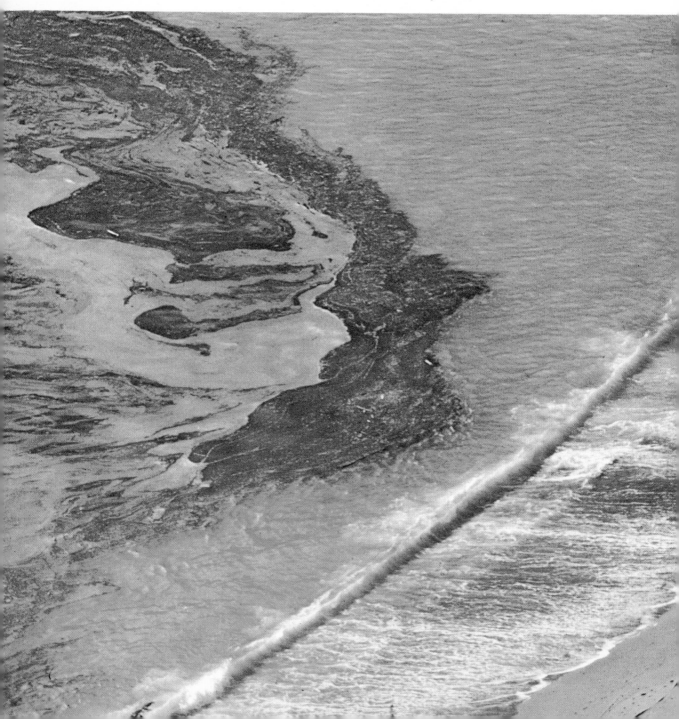

the amount of waste paper now being produced?

This approach lies behind some recent moves by enlightened consumer groups. Not long ago, more than 100 women, members of an organization called Friends of the Earth, entered a New York supermarket, did their weekly shopping, and took their baskets to the checkout counters, where they stripped every single piece of nonessential packaging from the goods they had bought and dumped it on the supermarket floor. This was, of course, only a token protest, but it was a dramatic way of attracting attention to the kind of social and industrial changes that may have to be made before we can hope to solve the enormous problem of pollution.

There have been similar protests elsewhere—nonreturnable bottles dumped on the manufacturer's doorstep in Britain, for example, or bottles of polluted river water sent to the Japanese government by angry Kobe citizens. And what lies behind them is a growing realization that pollution prevention and environmental protection cannot be brought forward by half-measures. Instead, our style of life, our methods

Left: the aftermath of a collision at sea. An oil slick drifts inshore at Kirby Cove State Park, California, from a holed supertanker. Accidents like this happen about once a day around the world. Above: a closer look at what happens to the beach when tons of clotted crude oil are deposited on the sand. By the use of emergency techniques and especially developed detergents, the sticky oil can be removed in a few months, but if left alone—as it often is—it will pollute the area for years.

17

of balancing the books, and our usual bland assumptions about economic growth and expansion must be completely changed.

Nature is intricately made up of biological communities of plants and animals that interlock into what is know as the ecosystem. This system can be subjected to limited abuse, from which it will in time recover, but persistent and large-scale abuse must bring about irreversible changes in the entire network. Man, who is a part of that network, deceived himself when he imagined that he could exploit the ecosystem for his own benefit and suffer no ill effects. He still deceives himself in many of his suppositions about the capacity of the ecosystem to absorb his pollution.

Even among those who understand how limited the earth's resources really are, there are many who believe that some kinds of pollution are not dangerous, because nature can easily cope with the relatively small amounts of pollutants. Thus they minimize, say, the seriousness of water pollution because they assume that the overall quantity of effluent has been very thinly spread throughout the world's vast supply of water. But this is not true. High local concentrations of poison frequently result in local ecological disruption, and this affects life for a long way up and down stream from the point of contamination. If we were dealing with simple physical or chemical systems, the problems would be fewer and less serious. But we are dealing with a total system that is incomprehensibly, delicately complex.

For instance, the bodies of living creatures can gradually accumulate thousands of times the concentration of contaminants found in their environment. On each step up the food chain, as a larger creature feeds on many smaller ones, the amount of accumulated pollutants in the body multiplies. A few years ago, the journal *Scientific American* carried a "food web" chart showing how just such a biological amplification had taken place in a Long Island estuary. The concentration of DDT in bay shrimps was only about 0.16 parts per million, but it rose to a massive 75.5 parts per million among the gulls of the area. There are predatory birds elsewhere in which the concentration of DDT has been found to be 1 million times as high as that in the waters where they obtain their food.

Does it really matter that materials such as DDT pass along the food chain—ultimately into human tissue—after they have been deposited

With at least 10 million tons of oil spilling into the seas every year, no living creature can be entirely free from the risk of contamination. The crab on the left was encrusted with oil as a result of an oil spill scores of miles out at sea. And the bird shown at below right could not know until too late that it was landing on an oil-covered rock after its flight over unpolluted water.

Hundreds of volunteers turned out to clear beaches after a recent oil spill near San Francisco, but willing help of this kind is no longer enough. While these and other men are raking local sands, and washing rocks and gulls' feathers, a thin film of oil and chemical waste is known to be building up on the surface of all the world's oceans. Nobody knows what this will eventually do to the natural environment of the sea, but it could have much more serious effects than a spill such as this one.

The detergent piled up here is a slimy testimony to man's assault on nature. Rivers have a great capacity for cleaning themselves; living organisms rid the water of many pollutants, and turbulence does the rest. But even Niagara Falls cannot disperse this residue.

Left: not very long ago, when 10,000 nonreturnable bottles were dumped on the doorstep of the London headquarters of a major soft-drink company, spokesmen for a group known as Friends of the Earth, which had organized the event in the best traditions of peaceful protest, were invited to discuss the problem with executives of the company. Pointing out that nonreturnable bottles not only create litter, but represent an obvious waste of resources, the protestors naturally suggested a readoption of the old system of returnable containers (on which the purchaser forfeits a cash deposit if he throws them away). But the company—not faced at the time with an immediate shortage of cheap raw materials for making bottles—felt unable to comply. Nevertheless, the publicity did some good for the antipollution cause, because it had the effect of attracting support for the Friends of the Earth's many similar campaigns.

Right: every day, thousands of tons of waste are poured onto this rubbish heap in New York City. Much of it is the remains of cooked or processed food, which attracts flies, rats, and birds. What such creatures do not scavenge—used engine oil, paper, plastic, and all the city's other assorted castoffs—is either burned (thus polluting the air) or plowed into the earth (polluting the soil and water).

in the ecosystem? The answer is certainly "Yes," Toxic chemicals are by definition poisonous. True, there are some naturally occurring poisons; but we know—even when we do not fully understand their mechanism—that they help to preserve the balance of nature. But DDT and similar compounds do not occur in man's natural environment, and they are likely to have *unbalancing* effects, even in minute dosages.

There are no known technological safeguards against pollution of this kind. And, even if there were, it seems likely that the consequences of biological disruption may not make themselves felt until they are so serious and far-reaching as to be beyond repair. For example, studies of the way water reaches us from underground sources suggest that some of us are now beginning to drink water that first entered deep aquifers—water-bearing rock formations—20 or more years ago. If this is so, it may be two decades before the toxic effects of agricultural chemicals in current use begin to take their toll.

From our experience with DDT, we ought by now to have learned that man-made "solutions" to environmental problems can be expected to create problems of their own. The gnats, flies, and mosquitoes that initially succumbed to DDT have been superseded—possibly *because* of DDT—by breeds that grow more resistant to the chemical with every dose. This in itself disturbs the natural ecosystem, leading to unforeseen effects. But we still continue to kill off various "pest" species or to change their roles in the ecological scheme. With our slender knowledge of many details of that scheme, we are putting ourselves at risk along with the insect pests.

Smog—a thick mixture of smoke and moisture—was once Britain's worst environmental problem. Much of it came from open coal fires, and cities such as Manchester (above) and London (left) produced so much that hundreds of people literally died of suffocation. The Clean Air Act of 1956 brought relief from this kind of pollution.

Because *all* life is threatened by some of man's actions, the problem of pollution is not a question of aesthetics or even of morals. It is a question of survival. The person who supposes that the battle against pollution can be won without basic social and industrial reforms may mean well, but he is unlikely to accomplish much by dealing with symptoms rather than causes. Oil spillage at sea is just such a symptom. Instead of concentrating on doing away with oil slicks, we might more profitably ask ourselves this enormous basic question: *Should massive energy resources be devoted to transporting colossal volumes of crude oil halfway around the world, so that it can be converted inefficiently into frequently trivial and polluting products, or can be used to produce power for similarly wasteful and completely unnecessary operations?*

Scarcely any official examination of the problems of pollution even hints that such questions need to be asked. Intelligent people in government, industry, the armed services, and elsewhere seem invariably to conclude that technological "progress" (whatever that means) must not be impeded. And they take it for granted that *more* manufacture, *more* trade, and *more* economic growth can be consistent with pollution prevention and environmental protection. In other words, people in positions of authority do not appear to have learned very much from past experiences with pollution control.

It seems almost too obvious to bear repeating that the pace of change and expansion in industrial societies is so fast that every device for alerting us to catastrophe rapidly gets out of date. So the polluting processes that we learned how to cope with yesterday are today superseded by less tractable ones. Or, in fact, the very methods of control may have brought on other problems. In the late 1950s, for example, the British Parliament passed a Clean Air Act that every sensible person supported. As a result of this law, industry's chimneys stopped pouring filth-laden smoke into the air, but Britain's *water* has suffered, for the smokeless-fuel industry that helped to diminish air pollution now pours

Too often, one solution brings on another problem. The horribly discolored waters above and the poisoned fish below are indirect casualties of Britain's well-intentioned Clean Air Act, which has led to the establishment of many large smokeless-fuel factories, whose highly toxic wastes have seeped into rivers.

copious and grossly toxic wastes into the rivers that pass its factories!

What we really need, then, is the kind of drastic environmental reform that can be achieved only by means of intense collective action. There is little that a single individual, or even a small group of well-disposed individuals, can do about it. An example springs to mind that is comparatively minor, but certainly relevant. I am typing the manuscript for this book in the manner preferred by publishers: double-spaced on only one side of the page. There seems to me to be no compelling reason why I should not cut paper, energy, and pollution costs by getting twice as many lines of type on both sides of every sheet of paper. But this would involve slightly more laborious operations at the printing presses, and every trend in today's world is from labor-intensive to energy-intensive operations. So my gesture would be a mere eccentricity. In fact, I should probably be requested to type the manuscript out again in the "right" way, thus wasting an even greater amount of paper.

So pollution is essentially a much broader social and political issue than many people realize. Most governments of the industrial nations have adopted environmental protection as an element of government policy, but the general view of what such a policy entails is extremely limited. As far as I know, no major political party in the world ever promises the electorate to carry out its environmental responsibilities by shifting the emphasis from economic growth (which by its very nature contributes to pollution) to a genuine effort to protect the environment through conserving and redistributing natural resources. The Soviet Union even takes the official line that the continuous creation of new technologies and the discovery of untapped resources will enable man to satisfy his increasing needs faster than his rate of population growth.

Although the Western democracies do not openly second this extremely bold statement, they behave as if they do. Unfortunately, however, all the available evidence indicates that such optimism is unwarranted. There can be little doubt that overexploitation and pollution stand as a barrier between humanity and its dream of a continuous, ever-broadening rise in material wealth.

In the following chapters we shall be looking at the various evidences of pollution in the modern world. I hope it is clear by now that there are many aspects of the problem, and so no single definition of the word "pollution" is likely to cover all of them. A well-known scientist has recently come about as close as possible to a definition by stating that pollution is "the addition to the environment, at a rate faster than the environment can accommodate it, of a substance or a form of energy (heat, sound, radioactivity, etc.) that is potentially harmful to life." One trouble with such an apparently sensible statement is that it can be seen as giving comfort to those who say that man is by nature a polluting creature. As some complacent people see it, the environment is indeed being changed, and always has been, through man's intervention—and a good thing, too! In the end, though, the definition trips up badly on that word "potentially." Any substance added to the environment "at a rate faster than the environment can accommodate it" is *certainly*, not just potentially, harmful.

The more one thinks about pollution, the more one realizes that there are so many qualifications involved, and so many allowances to be made, in an effort to comprehend what it is, that any all-embracing definition is sure to be inadequate. There was a time when I might have argued that pollution is, quite simply, a disruption of the environment that results from a self-serving, greedy use of the wealth of nature rather than a limited attempt merely to satisfy humanity's basic needs of food, clothing, and shelter. But that view is deficient in several respects. Cruelly feudal societies drew upon nature's capital without bringing about irreversible ecological changes; well-intentioned groups that lack scientific knowledge may harm the land through ignorance, not greed; and compassionate efforts to deal with disease and malnutrition can—and often have—badly upset the natural balances.

There are, however, some useful guidelines to what constitutes one or another kind of pollution. There are ideas worth pondering, too, about what might be done and what should not be done to avert disaster. We shall examine some of them after we have first looked at the nature and scale of the problem that faces us.

How two kinds of peppered moth—white (above) and black— have been affected by the smoke of British industry: the blacks, formerly rare because hungry birds spotted them easily on light-colored tree bark, became common when smoke blackened trees. Today, less smoke again means fewer blacks and more whites.

Pollution and Energy

In an industrial society we use energy rather as we use money. We change it from one currency to another, losing a little in "commission" with each such conversion, or we exchange it for goods, in which case we pay a little something extra to cover the "cost" of the transaction. To take a common example, we use the energy locked inside coal by converting it into electrical energy at the power station and conveying that electrical energy to our homes. There we change the electrical energy into heat energy in, say, an electric heater. If we burned the coal in a fireplace instead, for direct conversion into heat, we should lose a certain amount of energy—that is,

pay some "commission"—in the warmth that would be wasted by escaping up the chimney. But when we add to the number of conversions involved, we must pay not only the "commission" but a "cost" markup, for extra expenditures of energy are required in order to construct and run both the power station and our home equipment.

In nature, by contrast, there is no such thing as a waste product, and therefore, in theory, no "commission" to pay. Although an organism may produce matter that is redundant to its own survival, that matter will contain nutrients on which other organisms will live. The energy that goes into converting one material into another simply changes its form, and the overall balance remains constant. Take, for example, the process of photosynthesis, whereby green plants use the sun's energy for producing oxygen and organic material from water, carbon dioxide, and simple mineral salts. All the earth's oxygen is renewed

Although this generating station produces 2000 megawatts of electric power, it wastes more power than it produces, for much of its energy goes into the sky as steam lost through the cooling towers; construction and maintenance also consume energy. By comparison the windmill in the foreground, although it can generate only a few kilowatts, is much more efficient and less polluting.

Making gas from coal is a relatively efficient way to convert energy, provided that the heat can be usefully tapped during the process. But nothing approaches the efficiency of our major energy source, the sun—here seen rising over a typical gas plant.

in this way, and the radiation from the sun that the earth, with its plants, absorbs is balanced (or should be) by the radiation emitted back into space. Any major change would hurl us into another ice age or a world flood.

All energy, both natural and industrial, comes from the sun. Energy in the light that streams toward earth is stored in the atmosphere (in the form of water vapor and carbon dioxide), in the oceans (in the form of heat and microscopic organic energy systems), and on land (in the form

of heat and photosynthetic propagation). If most of this solar radiation were not ultimately re-radiated back into space, the earth would gradually be scorched to death. What the ecosystem does is to retain and circulate the amount of heat necessary to keep life in balance.

In humanity's constant quest for more energy, we may be putting this balance—and the planet—at great risk. The threat may seem remote, but it is nonetheless real. Is Alaska too far away for most of us to worry about what might happen

there as a result of oil production and transportation in the region? A spill of oil in the Beaufort Sea, northeast of Alaska, is capable of reducing the *albedo* (natural reflectivity) of large areas of the Arctic pack ice. The oil could emulsify into highly persistent droplets, which, circulated in the currents, would collect on the underside of the ice. After a few years, seasonal melting on top and freezing on the bottom would yield a darkened ice surface, and because black absorbs more heat than white does, the ice would melt more rapidly. A study of man's impact on climate indicates that the Arctic pack ice is already in an extremely delicate state and could be quickly melted by small climatic ups and downs. Far away? Perhaps—but the melting of Arctic ice packs would have profound and irreversible effects on the climate of the whole world.

The products of combustion in temperate-zone industry, borne on the winds, could just as easily settle on the ice, with similar effects. In any event, such products are already reaching the polar caps. Industrial pollutants and insecticides have been found in the tissues of penguins and fish in the Antarctic and of whales in the Arctic Ocean. No area is now free from contaminants that arise in the conversion of materials into energy or into other materials.

Such conversions usually involve the process of combustion—a natural process, to be sure, but a great squanderer of potential energy. For the act of industrial burning turns energy into scattered heat, noise, and friction, with accompanying mechanical losses, transportation-energy costs, and the production of pollutants. In other words, the energy goes up in smoke.

The problem is naturally most acute in the industrialized nations, where the generation of electricity accounts for a very high proportion of the fossil fuels (oil, coal, and gas) consumed. Thus we have the twin problems of pollution and the depletion of natural resources. Before the

typical power station generates any power, it throws away 10 per cent of its fuel energy through the stacks, because the flues have to be kept warm to prevent condensation of the steam that drives the turbines. A further 60 per cent of the remaining potential energy is lost through the conversion of heat energy to mechanical energy in the turbines, and then to electrical energy in the alternators. In other words, a 2000-megawatt station disposes of 4000 megawatts of warm water and steam. What the station wastes is energy in the form of "capital," because there can be no replacement of nature's hydrocarbon fuels once we have burned them up.

Inside and outside industry, by far the biggest spendthrift is the automobile. It consumes massive quantities of energy, largely in the form of raw fuel, but also in the various forms required for making, assembling, and maintaining its component parts and building highways, garages, parking lots, and service stations. In addition, it requires large energy "inputs" in the mining, refining, and processing of raw materials. And the car itself turns out to be the least satisfactory of all possible converters of energy.

About 5 per cent of the crude oils that are used for making base petroleum are lost in the refining process (mainly as simple pollutants and through spillage). Of what is left, 15 per cent disappears during its refinement into gasoline, and a further 5 per cent is lost in transport from the refinery to distribution and filling-station outlets. In other words, more than one fifth of its original energy has been effectively lost before the fuel is pumped into a car. As for the performance of the vehicle itself, estimates put the thermal efficiency of the engine at some 25 per cent, its mechanical efficiency at 70 per cent, and the efficiency of power transmission to the wheels at 70 per cent.

The resulting theoretical efficiency of a modern automobile as an energy converter, got by multiplying all the above figures together, is in the range of 10 per cent. But that is its energy-system efficiency only while it is purring steadily along the road in good physical condition. Slippage through poor transmission or driver control, through wear and tear, and through losses as a result of idling and sudden surges of acceleration reduces the figure to a staggeringly low efficiency of around 6 per cent!

Merely for direct use in keeping them on the move, the world's cars currently consume 6 per cent of our total production of energy. In terms of electric power, this amounts to between 4000 and 5000 million megawatt-hours a year. Much of it is going up quite literally in smoke—carbon monoxides, oxides of nitrogen, sulfur dioxide, hydrocarbon particulates, and lead. In bulk terms, the car now devours 12 per cent of the world's oil production and 5 per cent of its iron, steel, and major nonferrous metals (copper, lead, aluminum, and zinc). The United States uses more than half its oil to produce fuel for motor vehicles (mainly private cars); in fact, America devotes a higher share of fossil-fuel resources to the motor car than it does to meet all the rest of its vast commercial needs.

One form of energy waste that comes high on everybody's nuisance list is noise. And the noise of traffic is an overt and physically damaging type of atmospheric pollution. Most countries have set up objective anti-noise standards that must be met by new vehicles, but the laws are applied in a devil-may-care fashion—and, anyhow, most of the vehicles on the world's roads are comparatively old. The average age of all American cars in the mid-1970s was eight years; of European, 11. The older they are, the noisier the cars become, notably because of worn and corroded exhaust systems, but also because of mistimed and mistuned engines, defective insulation, and aging tires and transmissions.

But noise pollution, though hard on the nerves, remains a minor irritant compared with the major—and steadily worsening—menace of exhaust pollution. As long ago as 1964, well before the issue became as critical as it is today in many cities, a Paris police chief admitted that an increasing number of motorists who were being arrested for drunkenness were not drunk at all; they were suffering from the effects of carbon-monoxide poisoning! The city of Tokyo began to provide masks and respiratory aids for all traffic police, and decreed that those working at particularly busy intersections were to be relieved every hour on days of heavy traffic. After a photochemical smog hit New York City in 1970, the city's mayor warned that all private cars might soon have to be banned. And in Los Angeles, where two thirds of the total land space is given over to highways and parking facilities, the state legislature very nearly did ban so-called pleasure driving only a few years ago because of the smogs that the cars were causing.

The worldwide figures for exhaust emission are bad enough. For the United States alone they are colossal. U.S. traffic emits an annual total of 66 million tons of carbon monoxide, 12 million tons of hydrocarbons (virtually unburned oil and gasoline), one million tons of sulfur oxides, one million tons of heavy smoke particles, and large quantities of lead, derived from "antiknock" gasoline. Faced with all this, the American government has recently taken steps toward legislative control of all vehicle pollution and

33

Oil, our primary source of convertible energy, is also a primary source of pollution, not only when accidentally spilled from tankers and refineries, but at every stage of production and use. Above: immense amounts of energy are required merely for constructing rigs and drilling platforms such as this one, which is being prepared for operation in the North Sea. Right: "waste" oil is flared off the Alaskan coast at Cook Inlet, where, to get the oil, workers are changing a drill bit (below).

has established a major research program for more efficient engine design.

Complete control of exhaust emissions, however, is possible only with fairly complex, costly, and energy-intensive equipment, and sometimes the solution to the problem merely creates other problems. Quite apart from the high cost of additional engineering components, for instance, a car built to satisfy government standards for pollution-free vehicles would probably burn some 15 per cent more fuel than earlier models.

As in so many other areas of the pollution situation, the experts frequently disagree about the extent of damage to the environment and to humanity that can come from exhaust fumes. The British government's Transport and Road Research Laboratory has claimed that there are no toxic effects from carbon monoxide in the human body until a level of 10 per cent carboxy-hemoglobin in the blood has been reached. But other respectable authorities contend that poisoning can take place at one fifth of this level. Similarly, many official reports deny that the addition of lead to gasoline involves serious risks, but others indicate that the public is being slowly poisoned by the lead in traffic fumes. They say—with increasing support from independent studies—that such illnesses as impotence among men, brain damage, cardiovascular disease, fatigue, and chronic headaches are likely to occur with increasing frequency in places where automobile traffic is also increasing.

To ease the exhaust-fumes problem, engineers in the motor industry have been studying the possibilities of three main alternatives to the orthodox internal-combustion engine: the stratified-charge engine, the gas turbine, and the Stirling-cycle external-combustion engine. The first of these works on much the same principle as existing types; but instead of using an even air-fuel mixture, the charge is split up into levels of "richness" when it is ignited, and this theoretically produces a higher thermodynamic efficiency. Ford in America and Honda in Japan have been experimenting with the stratified-charge engine and claim significantly improved fuel-consumption figures and lowered levels of air pollution, but so far neither company has actually published its figures. The other two possibilities seem less practicable. In order to operate at sufficiently high temperatures, the gas turbine would probably need to be made of ceramic materials, and the Stirling-cycle engine would be very expensive.

In fact, any one of the three possibilities would require massive capital investment in retooling and would involve the use of very costly materials. Thus, they would need energy-intensive support to bring them into mass production. And the end result might well be disappointing, with little or no net energy savings and with only a slight change, if any, in the level of pollution created by gasoline-powered vehicles.

What about the alternative possibility of powering cars by rechargeable batteries? Well, it may sound fine if you give it only a moment's thought. But think further about the problem of maintaining all those batteries in a world that currently brings more than 22 million new cars on to the roads every year! Electric-car enthusiasts are promoting an idea that would probably exhaust the world's entire reserves of lead in about three years.

Even if a practical substitute for lead in batteries could be found, the change from oil to electric power would require the reconstruction of urban electric-power cabling, and would entail the annual erection of dozens of new electricity-generating stations. The responsibility for polluting the earth would merely be shifted from the cars themselves to these energy-hungry and energy-wasteful activities.

Some people who are determined to keep our profligate private-car-based transport system alive are pinning their hopes on cars driven by methane (from manure), by fuel cells (which combine active chemicals such as zinc and sulfur to produce electric current), or by steam. But these again ignore the energy-capital costs of producing the machines and all the supporting materials and systems for car-based transport. In the case of fuel cells, they jump economic and technological fences by unjustifiably assuming that the requisite chemicals will always be easily available, abundant, and cheap.

I have devoted a good deal of space to the energy and pollution problems created by cars because they provide an outstanding example of the shortsighted way we approach the whole question. Another equally glaring example is to be found in modern architecture. Today's buildings appear to be designed to make the most extravagant possible use of energy. Unnecessarily high lighting levels, poor thermal insulation, powerful air conditioning, electric heating, excessive volume, excessive use of such materials as cement and aluminum—reckless construction of this sort is perhaps best exemplified by New York's World Trade Center. This monstrous skyscraper is wired for 80 megawatts, and neither its

Left: status symbol, killer, gobbler of material resources, polluter—we can weigh the automobile's evils against its benefits. But most people in the industrialized world expect to own a car someday, and so do the inhabitants of many developing countries. For an idea of how such expectations are shaping our cities, we need merely glance at Los Angeles (above), where two thirds of all the city's space is devoted to the carriage or storage of cars—and where sunshine has been displaced by smog.

Architecture as an energy-intensive activity is embodied in New York's World Trade Center, an office complex wired for 80 megawatts of power—more than enough to supply a town of 50,000, but used here for a few thousand commuters. The energy costs of running this giant make it one of the world's most environmentally demanding buildings. At the other end of the scale is the Norwegian village where houses are built of low-cost and highly insulating materials. Small windows and thick walls help to conserve heating fuels; and although external pressures have raised energy demands for domestic appliances, transport, and so on, a settlement like this makes a comparatively modest call on resources—and creates little pollution.

butter after it comes out of the refrigerator. That sample of the West's thoughtless use of energy is worthy to stand beside the use of an electric heater to take the chill out of an air-conditioned room. But unless a ban is to be imposed on the manufacture, promotion, and sale of one or both of such counterbalancing appliances, the waste will continue. The typical purchaser is unwilling to give up his right to buy what he chooses just for the sake of reducing pollution.

And so our societies go on spending their energy capital; and the air we breathe, like the water we drink, becomes more and more tainted. There are, of course, a few individuals who adopt energy-saving programs of their own. It is questionable, however, whether individual efforts, no matter how dedicated, can arouse

society as a whole to the need for radical change. I know of a young architectural student who has built a self-sufficient house for his family. He is fairly typical of a small number of people who are striving to construct for themselves a non-polluting life style in—or, rather, outside of—the modern environment. Thus he is determined to have, in his words, "a house with its own energy system and its own waste-treatment plant, where you can grow your own food and tobacco and make your own wine and beer."

But although this young man has the good sense (and the ability) to use the wind to power his domestic electric generator, few of the rest of us are capable of building wind machines, even if we wanted to. How, then, *can* society cope with massive urban populations and their energy

41

Above: uranium mines such as this one in Gabon provide the world with what has long been regarded as the fuel of the future—a future when nuclear fission will have become a major source of electric power. Right: the control room of an atomic power station in Dresden, East Germany, sums up the technological splendor of it all.

needs without plundering nature and fouling the environment? Government-sponsored programs for exploring possible ways out of our dilemma are a prime necessity, and some have already been established. But to get an idea of the enormous scale of the problem, let us take a look at some of the territory now being explored.

Under consideration in recent years have been several possible power sources that might be less wasteful and less harmful to the environment than the fossil fuels. How much promise do they hold for the future? I shall suggest some answers to that question as we make a brief survey of the range of possibilities.

First, of course, there is nuclear fission. Splitting the uranium atom releases colossal energy, which could become useful heat under the controlled conditions of a fission reactor. In theory, this could provide the world with abundant, cheap, and clean power. Yet in Britain, where there were forecasts in the late 1940s of a completely nuclear-power economy by the mid-1980s, less than one tenth of the electricity of the mid-1970s was being generated in atomic reactors; and in the United States, after 25 years of research and development and the expenditure of billions of dollars, nuclear power had by 1975 only just surpassed firewood as a source of energy. What went wrong? What is holding us back? The answer is that the abundance, cheapness, and cleanness of nuclear power are, alas,

a matter more of theory than of practice.

We can have such power in abundance only if we also have the economic and technological capabilities to construct and maintain costly nuclear-power stations. The investment required "up-stream" in mining and processing enough uranium to cover a nationwide program would be stupendous. Even for a country as small as Britain, the enrichment capacity (necessary chemical preparation of the uranium) required for a 10-year period—assuming the same growth rate as that of present electric-power demands—would require an expenditure of $12,000 million. Nor is it simply a question of money. A tremendous number of physicists, chemists, engineers, and highly skilled manual workers would be essential for a full-scale nuclear-power program, for the operations of mining, processing, enrichment, and reprocessing are complex. So we should need a colossal specialist educational establishment to train the required manpower.

And would the system, if we finally got one, be nonpolluting? Nuclear fission is a technology in which, as someone has said, "no acts of God can be permitted." Even the most advanced and ingenious work in the field of safety engineering cannot guarantee full immunity from accidents, as several industrial and technological catastrophes during the past few years have proved. There is virtually no limit to the size of the disaster that might occur.

Below: in 1975, a fire at the world's largest atomic power station in Alabama put its supposedly fail-safe systems out of action. Growing numbers of accidents in such plants have been raising many doubts about nuclear-power technology, and opposition to the spread of atomic power plants is increasing.

There are incalculable risks in the containment of nuclear "raw material" and irradiated fuel—in the reactor, in transit, and in processing—and in the disposal of radioactive wastes. A variety of complex chemical, mechanical, electrical, and administrative accidents could mean disaster of unprecedented proportions. More than half America's nuclear reactors have been closed down for emergency checks in recent years. No completely fail-safe container for nuclear materials can be designed; neither can one that is invulnerable to theft or sabotage. And the dangerously radioactive life of nuclear waste products ranges from a minimum of 1000 years to one million. Thus, unless there have been some so-far-unpublicized major and novel advances in dealing with nuclear materials and radioactive wastes, it would seem that nuclear fission cannot yet provide a dependable, pollution-free substitute for the fossil fuels.

How about nuclear *fusion*, then? The prospect of extracting energy from the process of fusing nuclear material together at very high temperatures (as opposed to splitting individual atoms in the fission process) has long been a scientific and political white hope. There is no doubt that energy can be released in this way. What happens is that two hydrogen atoms are brought together to form one helium atom. In the process, which would have to be done under tremendously high temperatures, matter would be turned directly into energy, and—theoretically, at least—there would be no toxic by-products. Scientists are trying to achieve such a highly desirable result by containing the reaction inside powerful electromagnetic fields. If they are successful, they should be able to turn the hydrogen in one ton of water into the equivalent energy of 200 tons of coal or 60,000 gallons of gasoline.

But a general shortage of money, materials, manpower, and complex research equipment makes it extremely unlikely that the first prototype fusion reactor could appear before the end of the century. Success would no doubt be a giant step forward for mankind in our conquest of nature, but it remains possible that we could do a lot of harm by perfecting the fusion process. No one knows what risks are involved.

It is assumed, for instance, that there are no resource constraints on fusion because its raw material is deuterium, a form of hydrogen easily extracted from seawater. For all we know, however, deuterium may be biologically essential to the oceans, and wholesale extraction of it could seriously interfere with the natural balance of marine life. It would be unwise to rely on the promise of fusion before we find out what function deuterium performs in the sea. And so, although we are fairly certain that there would be neither operating risks nor poisonous by-products of nuclear fusion, too many mysteries remain unsolved for it to be seriously considered as a workable power source.

A third possibility—and one that *is* workable—is geothermal power (that is, power drawn from the natural heat of the earth). There are large subterranean reserves of usable heat, which can be tapped in the form of hot water and dry steam. Several such reserves are already being exploited. In California, one geothermal power plant now generates 275 megawatts of electrical energy and supplies it to two northern counties. Steam extracted from wells driven deep into the earth's crust is used for driving turboalternators. Engineers expect that in about five years the city of San Francisco will get all the power it needs from another such station located in the Imperial Valley. Similar plants are at work in Australia, New Zealand, and Italy. In general, they are less efficient than conventional power stations, but their construction, running, and maintenance costs are very much lower.

Geothermal energy has obvious drawbacks: it can be exploited only in geologically favorable places, and some of the heat is wasted when it is directly transmitted over long distances (one tenth may be lost for every 100 miles traveled).

Even the California example is a poor one in this respect, though a better alternative than present options. And there may be other, less immediately apparent drawbacks. So far, very little research has been done to establish how renewable this stock of energy might be, or whether and how it could be tapped in less obvious places. With much further research and technological advance, however, it might become a major power source, and a relatively nonpolluting one at that.

All the alternatives so far discussed—even, in a way, geothermal energy—are based on a withdrawal of capital from nature's limited supply of resources. The financial analogy makes good sense. It would surely be wiser to try to find ways to live on our income. So now let us examine the possible uses we can make of "income" energy—energy, in other words, that is continuously available in nature, and that would probably have the additional virtue of being largely nonpolluting.

To begin with, let us consider the relentless movement of the oceans. Tidal power has long been seen as a possibility, and many schemes for harnessing it have been advanced. The two major methods involve either the driving of generators by wave energy, or the storing of water at high tide and the use of its force as it runs back to sea at low tide. The problems, like those associated with most alternative energy sources, are underlined by the comparative shortage of research and practical development. Most informed opinion holds that tidal energy could provide no more than about one per cent of

No one is certain how much energy the world might actually be able to glean from the steam and hot water that lie just beneath the earth's crust, but a number of countries are already exploiting the power of their geothermal wells. If untapped by man, the steam loses its force, simply escaping into the atmosphere from geysers like the one above at Rotorua in New Zealand. But at Wairakei (left), 40 miles away, a large power plant runs on controlled steam from nearby wells.

45

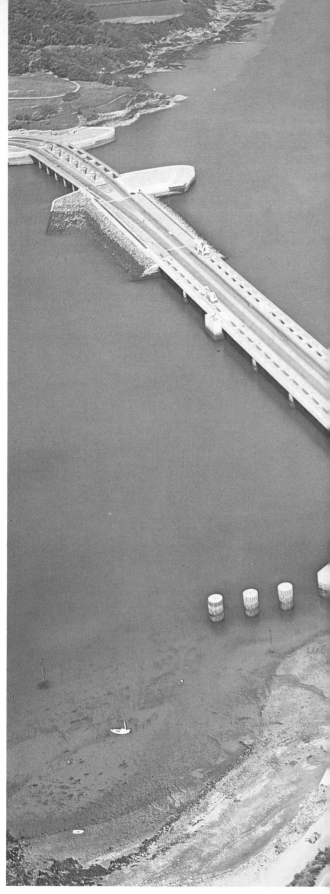

Man's dream of harnessing the tides is an old one; schemes for doing so go back to Roman times. Modern suggestions involve converters that would turn wave motion into rotary power by mechanical means. More ambitious projects, such as the tidal barrier at Rance in France (right), store up the energy in trapped water, but they may be more costly than effective.

the power that might be made available from ordinary hydroelectric stations. In view of the limited research so far, though, we cannot be sure that this pessimism is justified.

A few tidal-energy plants are already operating, in France (at Rance) and in North American (at Passamaquoddy in Maine and Canada). From their experience we can see the outstanding disadvantages of tidal power. Large systems do not pollute the air, but they affect local geography and alter local geology and ecology. Plant and shellfish communities are disrupted, the shoreline changes, wind and rain patterns are modified, and shipping and fishing patterns in the area are endangered. Construction costs are enormous, too. When entirely completed, the Passamaquoddy scheme is likely to have cost a good deal more than the $650-million estimate made in 1973. Yet it will generate no more than 500 megawatts—a low return for a very high price. Unless simpler, less costly construction

techniques are devised, development of such schemes is therefore likely to remain limited.

There are other, more traditional ways to use water power, of course. Water is one of our oldest energy sources; it still supplies mankind with more than one tenth of his total energy demands, and with a much larger proportion of his total electrical requirements. According to most estimates, however, all the really favorable hydropower sites are already being exploited. For a significant rise in overall output, there would have to be some "reinforcing" technologies—more efficient water turbines, better dams, and so on. Even then, we should need to solve several other problems in order to have bigger, more widespread, and more productive hydroelectric plants.

For example, we have not yet learned how to cope with the accumulation of river-borne silt that eventually makes most man-made reservoirs useless. And once again we must face up to the menace of ecological damage. Recent experience with very large dams, especially in tropical countries, suggests that the side effects—on climate, fishing, plant life, and health—may make them a poor bargain. And so the largest current projects—notably those planned for Arctic rivers (which would be diverted to vast reservoirs in Siberia)—are being delayed pending further research into their probable effects on the environment and the climate.

Finally, and perhaps most promising, is the power to be drawn from our inexhaustible fund of sunlight. Solar energy can be tapped either directly or indirectly. As we know, the sun's energy is stored and passed through all organic systems. Thus we are indirectly using it in such undertakings as agriculture, forestry, fishing, hunting, and so on. In theory, then, it should be possible to build artificial energy systems that would use the same principles as those that govern the process of photosynthesis. We do not yet know how to do this, though, and it is unlikely that we shall in the foreseeable future.

A much more feasible energy source that comes indirectly from solar power is a familiar one, the wind. In theory, the wind could provide enough inexhaustible sources of energy to fulfill all our needs. One scientist has calculated that the winds, if they could be harnessed, might turn out twice as much electricity as water power does now. In fact, though, it is unlikely that they could ever provide the power for more than a few

Left: Nevada's Hoover Dam is an impressive example of how the world's inland waters can provide hydroelectric power as part of linked projects for irrigation. In general, hydropower is a clean, low-impact technology; the light, airy turbine hall at the Bonneville Dam in Oregon (above) exemplifies this comparatively nonpolluting supply of energy.

Top right: conservation before exploitation. Giant stone sculptures at Abu Simbel were removed to high ground before Egypt's Aswan Dam was flooded. Bottom right: in a wildlife variation on the same theme, rhinos were rescued before the flooding of Rhodesia's Kariba Dam. In both cases, however, damming may have harmed the environment.

small, individual needs, for they are uniquely fickle, depending on any number of unpredictable factors, including the seasons, the climate, and local topography. As I have indicated, some unconventional builders are mounting wind machines on the roofs of "autonomous" houses. Such machines are certainly useful for driving electric generators, and recent experiments suggest that they might also help to heat water directly by simply churning it. So they may some day be important contributory factors in larger power systems. But they are most unlikely, in view of their undependability, to become more than merely contributory.

On the other hand, nothing in our world is more dependable than direct solar energy. Every *second*, the sun converts 587 million tons of hydrogen into 583 million tons of helium. The missing 4 million tons are discharged into space, mainly in the form of heat and light, and the earth receives about one part in every 2000 of these rays. Most of the potential as a direct power source goes unexploited, but the severity of the energy crisis has spurred intensive research into ways and means of turning direct solar energy into the power that the developed nations want. The U.S. National Science Foundation alone has been spending about $30 million a year on the quest for relatively inexpensive solar-power systems, and work is also under way in Japan (where dependence on imported oil is a spur to a search for alternative power sources).

"Free" income-type energy from the sun could, in theory, provide the world with a boundless supply of virtually pollution-free power. But conversion on a large centralized scale seems a less likely prospect than conversion in small units— one for each building or group of buildings. Some such units are already functioning, to produce hot water and, through heat pumps (rather like

refrigerators in reverse), heating and air-conditioning systems. The technologies for small-scale conversions are, surprisingly enough, quite simple. Black-surface collectors that catch the sun's rays and pass the heat into water can reach very high temperatures in quite cloudy weather; one such private installation in London heats water to 130°F even on the overcast days of an English March. To learn how to turn sunlight directly into heat or electricity on a significant scale, however, would need further research.

Still, initial investigations are promising and suggest that capital costs are likely to be well within the means of the world community. Widespread photothermal conversion (sunlight-heat-electricity) would use up a great deal of space for the solar-collection panels—but much less, in fact, than, say, prolonged strip-mining of coal. And some American authorities believe that the transition from theory to practice may

Wind, an indirect form of solar energy, has served man well in the past, and it could be much further developed as a nonpolluting power source wherever the right conditions prevail. Modern scientists are stepping up research into more efficient ways of catching the wind and storing the power it can generate. Conventional windmills, such as those that power this water-pumping station in Majorca, continue to do their job well. And vessels such as the Statsraad Lemmkuhl *(above), which competed in a recent Tall Ships race, can give many a diesel-powered craft a run for its money when the wind is right.*

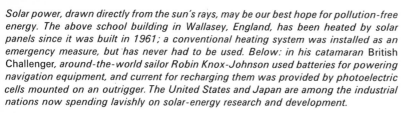

Solar power, drawn directly from the sun's rays, may be our best hope for pollution-free energy. The above school building in Wallasey, England, has been heated by solar panels since it was built in 1961; a conventional heating system was installed as an emergency measure, but has never had to be used. Below: in his catamaran British Challenger, around-the-world sailor Robin Knox-Johnson used batteries for powering navigation equipment, and current for recharging them was provided by photoelectric cells mounted on an outrigger. The United States and Japan are among the industrial nations now spending lavishly on solar-energy research and development.

not be too far off. U.S. government research teams have recommended the early construction of "solar farms"—large electricity-producing solar-power stations—which would be equipped with huge radiation collectors.

Properly handled, direct solar energy holds out genuine promise of a practically pollution-free source of power. Of almost equal importance is the fact that, by offering fair shares to almost every corner of the habitable world, it would reduce the risk of an energy war. But even solar energy would present society with a truly epoch-making choice. On the one hand, we could use it to intensify the feverish pace of industrialization and urbanization; on the other, we could employ it as part of a whole new culture based on low-impact technologies. Having at last developed a cheap, safe, and clean source of energy, would mankind be capable of managing it so as to prevent serious ecological and climatic damage? Or should we use our vast new reserves of power to carry on even more recklessly?

At any rate, none of the other energy sources

At this "solar farm" high in the French Pyrenees, 63 giant panels track the sun as it moves across the sky, and bounce its rays onto a 148-foot-high parabolic reflector (below). From the reflector— actually the especially treated side of an office building—the light is focused into a "solar furnace" located in the small structure immediately in front. Temperatures as high as 6300°F (hot enough to burn a hole through armor plate) have been recorded. Ideally, this heat could be converted into electrical energy; at present, however, it all goes to waste.

that I have been discussing is likely to provide us with a satisfactory substitute for the fossil fuels before we are well into the 21st century. Until then we must continue to draw on our "capital" resources: oil, coal, and natural gas (products, of course, of indirect solar collection billions of years ago).

About 97 per cent of the world's primary energy is now being derived from these fuels: 38 per cent from coal, 40 per cent from oil, and 19 per cent from natural gas. And the rate of depletion for each of these is always increasing.

Attempts to calculate how long our reserves of fossil fuels will last are full of uncertainties. But it seems likely that if consumption patterns do not change, if refinery technologies do not significantly advance, and if huge geological surprises do not lie ahead, we are going to be more than halfway through total world reserves of crude oil by the year 2000. Coal should last considerably longer (and with it the problem of how to make its mining socially and environmentally acceptable). As for natural gas, it is not only in

A natural balance exists between the protection given by the earth's atmosphere against too much sunshine and our need for enough light to keep life going. When we interfere with upper atmospheric layers by polluting the air, we may drastically affect that delicate balance, and the earth could become intolerably hot, or—if the disruption took a different turn—winter might last all year.

relatively short supply, but it is costly to transport and, when liquefied, involves large environmental hazards. When spilled on water, as it might be if a liquefied-gas tanker were to collide with another boat, the low-temperature fluid boils immediately, releasing a ground-level cloud of asphyxiating methane. On land, a spark—even contact with a running car engine—could turn a carrier of the fluid into an enormous incendiary device, which might ignite an entire port and industrial complex.

To sum up, our fossil fuels are variously vul-

nerable to economic crisis and political pressure, in relatively short supply, and difficult to control environmentally. In fact, we simply do not know the long-term environmental effects of burning oil, coal, and gas. All combustion from the fossil fuels produces carbon dioxide (among other gases) and emits it into the atmosphere, where it has been steadily increasing at an annual rate of about two parts in every 1000. Half this accumulation of CO_2 remains in the air, which could, in theory, be completely filled with it in 700 years; the other half goes into the biosphere and the

climate, but an example from natural history shows how truly staggering the effects might be.

In 1815, the eruption of Mt. Tambora on the island of Sumbawa in Indonesia threw an estimated 90 cubic miles of ash up into the atmosphere. In 1816, there was no summer worth the name in either the northern United States or northern Europe; in England the mean temperature for July, which had been established over 250 years of record-keeping, dropped from 59.1°F to 56.1°F, a drastic fall, and one that, if prolonged, would significantly alter plant and animal behavior. Temperatures in the Northern Hemisphere have been dropping steadily in recent years, and it is possible that man's constant injection of small particles into the atmosphere is at least one of the causes. Colder weather is only one of the worldwide consequences of industrial pollution from energy-conversion processes. At the same time, new buildings and roads are reducing green-plant cover on the earth's surface, thus diminishing the amount of free oxygen in the air; and the burning of fossil fuels has added 15 per cent to the atmosphere's carbon dioxide in the last 100 years, with the percentage still rising.

Our lavish production of thermal effluents has brought about all these changes in the contents of the atmosphere, and we do not know the meteorological and climatic outcome. It is possible that we may not even detect disastrous trends until they have gone too far. In the process of "improving" our lot on earth, we may already have permanently disrupted the finely tuned natural-energy balance.

In barely two centuries of industrialization, modern man has meddled with the earth's energy budget to such an extent that, according to one environmental scientist, the way may be opening up for the development of entirely new ecological regimes that could conceivably exclude man and the more complex life forms. To such an end—if this were indeed to be the end—man would have survived a few hundred years of steady industrialization. During that short period he would have bankrupted his capital energy sources, engaged in worldwide conflict in the search for more, and created the conditions for terminal human misery on an unprecedented scale. In one way or another, the environment will eventually repair itself. But our descendants will live to see it only if we begin to act *now* for our own benefit and theirs.

oceans—in what proportions no one is sure.

The growing amount of carbon dioxide in the atmosphere has what is known as a "greenhouse" effect, trapping and concentrating the heat derived from the sun. This might be expected to lead to a gradual rise in the earth's temperature, and thus to climatic change. But—and it is a big "but"—the greenhouse effect seems to be more than offset by the opposing impact of atmospheric dust created by the modern world's agriculture and industry. Apart from ordinary dust, the atmosphere contains combustion-produced sulfates, nitrates, and hydrocarbons, all of which may stay in the lower stratosphere as small particles for as long as three years. We have little accurate knowledge of their effect on

Pollution and Agriculture

In the continuing debate about our environment, no aspect of the subject generates more heat and confusion than the question of pollution as it relates to farming. One thing is certain: most of us in the West frequently forget that we owe nearly everything we have to the land. The land provides us not only with most of our food but also with shelter, clothing, and the energy required for running our machines.

It is easy to overlook our dependence on the land, of course, for we live increasingly in cities, and we depend on advanced technologies that conceal our ultimate reliance on the soil and what lies beneath it. Even the name we give to the products we use may often mask their origins. The term "man-made fibers," for example, does not immediately remind us that we must wrest crude oil from the ground in order to make the polymers from which to manufacture synthetic textiles. To a society such as ours, oil is as much a "farmed" commodity as wheat—and it has become as essential. So it is impossible to exaggerate the importance of agriculture to man.

By the mid-1970s, however, the world's farming appeared to be in poor shape, with too many people chasing too little of everything. Several factors conspired to make the situation a serious one. The first was the steady growth of the world's population, with some 80 million more mouths to feed every year. The second was a succession of disappointing harvests in the major agricultural countries—a result mainly of bad weather (which may itself have been partly brought on by man's impact on the climate). There was also a strikingly rapid rise in oil prices, and thus in the costs of farm machinery and oil-based fertilizers. But although we were forced to ask the disturbing question, "Can we produce enough farm products to satisfy the world's needs?" an equally vital question became (and remains), "What are the environmental consequences of attempting to do so in the way that we are following at the moment?"

These consequences as they affect our food supply alone could be the most serious that humanity has ever had to face. They fall into four main categories, dictated by (1) the energy requirements of modern farming, (2) the use of

fertilizers, (3) the use of pesticides and herbicides, and (4) the large-scale alteration of soil structures brought on by large-scale farming methods. Although food is basically produced as a result of solar energy, it is now grown in the West with the help of a whole range of technologies that are designed to increase crop yields. The resultant yields should theoretically exceed those obtainable from simple natural systems. But even if they do, agricultural pollution and contamination of foodstuffs, of surface waters, and of the entire biosphere stem largely from our use (or misuse) of the new technologies.

Let us begin by examining the part that

To farm these wheat fields in the rich soil of the State of Washington, it has become an economic necessity to tap a good many other resources first: oil, iron ore, rubber, and all the various materials required for today's highly mechanized agriculture. But mechanization means pollution, and it may become economically unprofitable as the world's limited supplies of fossil fuels and metals dwindle and their costs rise. Our dilemma is that most of us no longer live and work where we ourselves could harvest our own grain and tend our beasts of burden in the "primitive" old way (left). Nevertheless, there are signs of a limited attempt to do just this; in Britain, for instance, several hundred farmers are known to have exchanged their machines for horses during the last few years, thus reversing a trend nearly a century old.

57

agriculture plays in the present world energy situation. At the beginning of the century, a roughly equal number of men and horses together provided the main energy input to farming. Where farmers were concerned, electrical power, the internal-combustion engine, and advanced chemicals were practically unheard-of. By the middle of the century, however, few beasts of burden still worked in the fields of the developed countries, and the number of machines employed on the land had overtaken the number of laborers. During the intervening years, the power input to the land had increased roughly six times.

It has been calculated that in some Western countries today, 300 horsepower-hours a year are devoted to every machine-worked acre of grass and crops. Assuming that the machines have an overall efficiency rate of 33 per cent—a very liberal estimate—and that a real horse used to perform about 1500 hours of work a year, the con-

sumption of energy in modern farming represents the deployment of one horse for every five acres, as compared with one for 25 to 30 acres at the turn of the century! In simpler terms, we are using more to obtain less—putting more energy into the production of food than is effectively recovered in the form of protein. As we saw in the preceding chapter, this amounts to an expenditure of capital, not, as in days of old, of income.

The degree of energy wastage varies at different points in the system—from oil fields to wheat fields, for instance—and depends on the type of crop and the quality of soil involved. Generally such wastage takes the form of the products of combustion, which, with dust, add to the polluting load on the atmosphere. And the more we use capital energy, the less effective it proves in raising the output of healthy crops. Modern agricultural methods in the West require about 250 times as much raw energy per acre in

Below: this picture of a battery henhouse in Brazil is a striking illustration of the way the basic techniques of farming have changed. Few farmers claim to like this kind of factory rearing, and no one imagines that the hens like it, but it has become an "economic necessity," with the birds fed from high-volume meal industries, and their produce going to densely populated cities.

mechanical and chemical form as China needs for her rice farming. This is largely because no energy-exchange cycle is basically more sound than the natural cycle, with its use of manure fertilizer. What we are discovering is a law of diminishing returns in the use of nitrogenous fertilizers, which are industrially produced compounds based on nitrogen, phosphorus, and potassium, and of which we now spread millions of tons on our farmlands.

The energy requirements for producing this artificial fertilizer are enormous. Almost one third of the total energy input for growing potatoes, for example, goes into fertilizers. A survey of a recent 15-year period indicates that the farmers of the Western world increased their yields by 34 per cent during that period. But at the same time they increased their yearly expenditure on tractors by 63 per cent, their annual investment in fertilizers by 146 per cent, and their bulk requirements of chemical pesticides by 300 per cent. The same survey concludes that a further 34 per cent increase in food production would demand even greater inputs of energy, which would mean still more pollution from the conversion processes involved.

All the modern technologies that are applied to the land—machines, fertilizers, weed killers,

Above: farm life was hard a century ago, when milking was a chore. Sometimes the cows gave infected milk, and their yield was unreliable. Below: in the computerized milking parlor of a modern farm, by contrast, a herd can be attended to by one man with little effort, and the milk is clean and plentiful. But who can assess the enviromental costs of "processing" domestic beasts?

pesticides, dairy detergents, propionic acid for grain preservation—make inroads into our capital supply of energy. All of them demand fossil-fueled power and factories for their production. And in most cases it looks as though we shall soon have almost nothing to show for our pains. For example, Japan uses seven times as much pesticide as the U.S., but it produces only twice as much per acre. Europe gets twice the crop yields common in Africa, but at an expense of 11 times as much pesticide. The same discrepancies occur when we look at figures for the use of fertilizer. They are disturbing not simply because they remind us of the great risks of pollution from such widespread and large energy exchanges, but also because modern technology depends on oil, an increasingly scarce commodity.

No one doubts that the world's farmers have stepped up their use of fertilizers in good faith. Because of the pressures of population and the shift away from specializing in leguminous plants (peas, beans, and so on), which were the centerpiece of the agricultural revolution of the 18th century, the farmer has gone in for using a form of fertilizer that can be very rapidly assimilated by his crops.

Ordinarily, plant nutrients would be superabundant in the atmosphere, in the soil, and in animal manure. But because people of the developed countries have become increasingly fond of meat—and capable of affording it—the farmer now depends on artificial fertilizer, so that he can concentrate on the high-speed growth of grains suitable for animal feed. And with this

Farming in the wetlands of the Far East still depends on fertile soil and the labor of man and beast. Although these rice fields in Bali yield as much food per acre as any land in the world, they get less than 0.5 per cent of the mechanical power applied to Western farms, and so they do far less damage to the environment.

dependence on chemical fertilization, he has been allowing animal manure to pass into rivers and streams rather than onto the fields.

When industrially produced fertilizers were first introduced, it was thought that the minerals would dissolve in rainwater and would be entirely absorbed by plant roots. It now appears that this was a fairly serious oversimplification, for the effectiveness of any fertilizer depends very much on the soil. All soil contains tiny microorganisms; these are associated with the organic condition of the soil, which in turn gives it its structure and strength. Large doses of chemical fertilizer reduce the organic strength, affect the natural availability of nutrients, and have an adverse effect on the microorganisms in the soil. On the one hand, then, chemical fertilization

reduces the capacity of the soil to make nutrients for itself; on the other, it tends to break down the soil by reducing its organic content. For a time, at best, it may help the inefficient farmer to stay in business, but *only* for a time.

Thus, we can justifiably define modern fertilizers as potential contaminants. An organic content of 8 per cent in the topsoil used to be considered very nearly essential for arable land. In many areas today, the organic content is down to 3 per cent, mainly because of the stripping effects of various kinds of fertilizer.

At the same time, there is mounting evidence that the chemical fertilizers act as direct pollutants further along the ecological chain. As large quantities of nitrates and phosphates are washed off the land, they enter freshwater

This farmer in Nepal plows his land in what looks like an intolerably primitive fashion. But the clumsy plow, low speed, and natural—rather than chemical—fertilizer will probably keep his land richer than the mechanically cultivated soils of the West.

systems—lakes and rivers—where they so enrich the waters that there is a large increase in biological activity. The resultant imbalance in local biosystems eventually kills off parts of such systems. This phenomenon, which brings on a choking surface accumulation of plant life and weed cover, is known as *eutrophication.*

Under natural conditions, eutrophication may be expected to develop after rivers and streams have washed millions of years' accumulation of salts downstream. Modern agriculture has greatly accelerated the process; it is estimated, for instance, that America's farmers—greatly aided, to be sure, by industrial operations—have "aged" Lake Erie 15,000 years before it would have happened naturally. Thus, one of the Great Lakes is effectively dead—so contaminated that not even boiling will render its water drinkable. And when this sort of thing happens, the biological repercussions in the rest of the lake or river system are not hard to imagine. The unnaturally extensive plant cover devours oxygen, leaving precious little for the sustenance of fish and animal life.

But the danger of overusing chemical fertilizers does not stop here. The nitrates in fertilizer may also be a threat to human health. We have seen that there are limits to how far the farmer can increase the yield of his land by the use of fertilizers. There is a point beyond which you cannot "push" a crop, but today's farmers have got themselves into a fix wherein they are economically obliged to employ more and more nitrogenous fertilizer in order simply to keep production at a steady level. U.S. farmers are now using four times as much fertilizer as they were just after World War II for each unit of crop grown! The question arises, if the increased amounts of nitrogen are not going into the crop, where *are* they going? And the simple answer is that they are going into our drinking water (as well, of course, as into the sea).

In themselves, nitrates are not poisonous. Once inside the intestine, however, they can be converted into nitrites, which combine with blood chemicals to form a compound called methemoglobin. This inhibits the circulation of oxygen through the bloodstream and brings on a well-known condition called methemoglobinemia, which suffocates some farm animals, and that may produce so-called "blue babies" among human beings. We do not yet know for certain whether there is a direct link between our use of inorganic fertilizers (as opposed to organic ones such as manure) and the incidence of methemoglobinemia. But there are good grounds for concern. Surely we should pause before going ahead with plans—as in the United States—for increasing the use of chemical fertilizer 10-fold between now and the year 2000?

Much of our drinking water comes from chalk and sandstone aquifers—natural underground reservoirs that provide water for more than half

The droppings from such birds as these cormorants and pelicans on the Chincha Islands off the coast of Peru used to form a major source of fertilizer for the world's farmers, who now rely on petrochemical fertilizers—an energy-wasteful cause of pollution.

the population in some countries. Until fairly recently, geologists believed that these aquifers receive rainwater that has filtered through the earth's surface, and that they yield it up again in a matter of weeks or, at most, months. It was therefore assumed that the water that emerges at springs and bore holes is of fairly recent origin, and that any contamination from nitrates would become quickly apparent. The risk of such contamination seemed minimal, because none showed up in analyzed samplings of water.

In the past few years, however, there has been an unexplained increase in the nitrate level in water that was previously free of nitrates. The possibility that this could result from the use of artificial fertilizers seemed remote as long as we believed that water emerges from aquifers within weeks of being received; after all, nitrogenous fertilizers had been in vastly increasing general use since the end of World War II, and there had been no trace of nitrogen in the water until recently. But we now know better. Research carried out by means of radioactive tracers that follow the course of water through aquifers has revealed that the water can take more than 20 years to complete its journey through the soft rock beneath the earth's surface. And so we are faced with the very real possibility that public water supplies are steadily growing more tainted with nitrates, reflecting the fertilizer usage of the past few decades. Even in a country such as Britain, with its exceptionally high standards for

Above: Lake Erie has been killed by a massive load of industrial and farm pollutants. Fish that enter it from tributary streams die, starved of oxygen in the weed-choked water. In the words of one ecologist, "It's too thick to drink, too thin to plow."

Above: environmental degradation has increasingly become the subject of literature, music, and the visual arts. This sculpture entitled "Pollution" is to be seen on the shore of Lake Ontario.

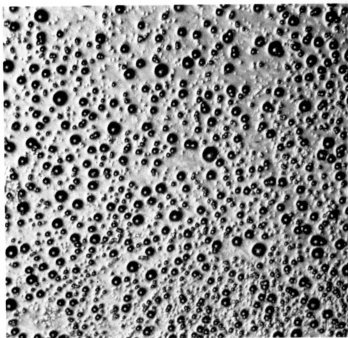

Above left: the Indiana Harbor Ship Canal is now no more than a ribbon of oil and slime that flushes through East Chicago. Oil refineries and steel mills are the main polluters, but runoff from farmland contributes. *Above right:* a close-up of the canal.

water quality, nitrate levels during the last five years have occasionally exceeded those laid down as safe limits by the World Health Organization. In the developing countries, where controls are less stringent, the danger may be even greater.

When we consider the whole tangled question of fertilizers, farming, and food, we are confronted by massive contradictions that are by no means easy to resolve. Although we may be keenly aware of the pollution risks to which we are exposing ourselves, we cannot simply return to an agricultural society in which there are no machines and no complex chemicals. Even if we wanted to do this, the backward shift would bring with it other social changes so far-reaching as to be at present unthinkable. Imagine what would be the consequences of a universal decision to dismantle chemical plants and lay off their employees, to shut down tractor-assembly lines, and to prepare for the breeding of millions of horses! The best we can do, perhaps, is to carry on a good deal more cautiously with mechanization and the use of chemicals, always trying to make sure that the benefits outweigh the disadvantages, always listening to those who may disagree with the "wisdom" of the day.

And we should probably adopt a similar attitude toward pesticides and herbicides. In the early days, a few voices were raised against their indiscriminate use; but most industrialists, economists, and agriculturists regarded them as essential substances for an age of plenty, and so they took little notice of the critics. For one thing, business and industry had invested millions in the equipment for manufacturing these chemicals, and no investor, whether large or small, wants to listen to those who say he has spent his money foolishly or to society's disadvantage. The news media largely took the same view and, because there are not many journalists with scientific training, gave little coverage to critics who—for all the newsmen knew—might be merely cranks and troublemakers. As a result, there were few early curbs on farmers' efforts to get rid of pests and weeds, with some disastrous effects on the environment.

A lot depends on how we define an agricultural "pest." From the earliest and most primitive beginnings, farmers have exercised simple controls over "pests" and "weeds"; various plants and animals have fallen in and out of these categories as the farmer has learned more and as methods of food production have advanced. By

the end of the 19th century, in fact, farmers had achieved a high degree of control merely by careful manual husbandry and the intelligent organization of their crops. The introduction of row-drilling in the 18th century, coupled with the development of very efficient seed-handling—the old seedsmen were among the most reliable and fastidious merchants ever—meant that the fields on many a farm 100 years ago were remarkably close to being free of weeds.

Then came mechanization and, later, single-crop cultivation. Deterioration set in, and the conditions were established for a farm system in which chemical pest control would seem to be ever more essential. An increasing number of living creatures came to be regarded as "pests." In the distant past, the real pests had been mammals that preyed on farmers' herds, but on a

Above: crop-dusting biplanes fly over lettuce fields near Mesa, Arizona. Although selective pesticides have been developed, the chemicals used in exercises like this one often kill useful plants and wildlife as well as the pests for which they are intended. The picture gives some idea of the scale of one-crop culture now common in the Western world; it actually encourages the concentration of hardy pests in a single area.

Right: one of the aftereffects of indiscriminate crop-spraying: a deciduous forest has been laid waste by airborne pesticides. The land has now been partly replanted with conifers, but these trees are chiefly of immediate use to man, and have a limited value as a wildlife habitat.

highly specialized farm today a butterfly or a wild flower becomes a pest—technically, at least—if it feeds on crops, reduces yield, or in any way upsets the farm's economics. Bombarded with advice and pressures from a variety of sources such as governments, chemical suppliers, farmers' unions, housewives, and so on, the modern farmer is sure of only one thing: he must grow more and more, simply to stay in business. To do this he has concentrated on single crops, whereas once he mixed a great variety and probably ran a dairy herd too. And he has vastly stepped up his reliance on technological aids.

Many of the agricultural pests that now seem to be such a problem are there because we have created the conditions in which they proliferate. When you eliminate one insect, the smaller creatures that it used to eat begin to multiply.

You then eliminate those, and so on; there is a "cascade" effect. It also happens that after a field has been sprayed to kill off a specific insect, others less susceptible to the insecticide begin to flourish. In effect, they have been inoculated against the chemical, or have at least built up a resistance to the original dose. Meanwhile, the spray may have killed off *their* natural enemies. So a whole chain reaction of disturbances can be set off, with beneficial organisms dying and the pests surviving in greater numbers than before.

In America, the number of harmless organisms that pesticides have seriously damaged is large. Apart from insects, those accidentally killed off in sprayed areas have been known to include robins, whitefish, earthworms (among the farmer's most useful natural allies), ducks, rabbits, quail, trout, foxes, opossums, mice, ospreys, pheasants,

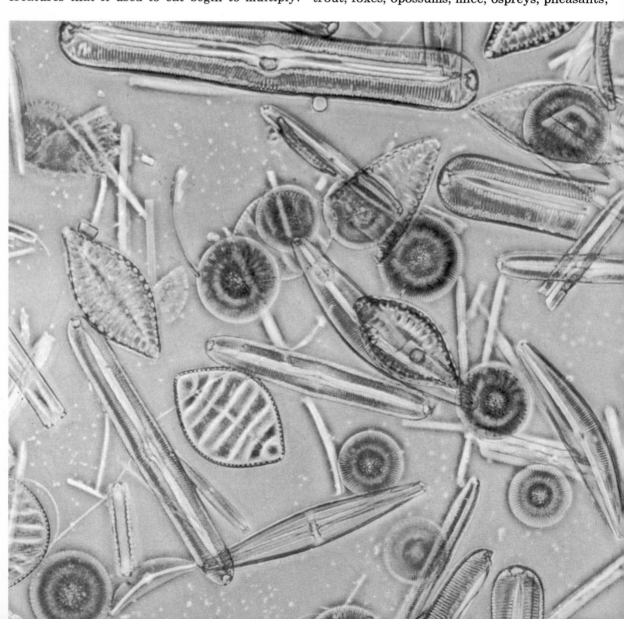

turkeys, seagulls, crabs, salmon, snakes, and muskrats. Any significant poisoning of such animals affects the environments in which they have lived. It also threatens us, for as toxic chemicals pass upward in the animal kingdom, their concentrations can multiply rapidly from creature to creature, and because everything we eat or drink is vulnerable to chemicals, there are bound to be risks to our own health.

One insecticide that has been in common use on the farms of the Western world—endrin—is known to produce symptoms of dropsy (liver cancer, hypertension, brain damage) in fish. Its use has now been curtailed, but the effects may be persistent, and may reach man through the food chain. And endrin is only one of hundreds of chemical pesticides that, until very recently, were freely sold to farmers.

It is sometimes claimed that only chemical controls stand between humanity and starvation or death from insect-borne disease. But in many cases recently examined, the reverse seems true. Even in small and localized doses, insecticides can deal death on a wide scale to essential living organisms. For instance, DDT, possibly the best-known insecticide, affects marine life many miles from its place of use and in concentrations of only a few parts in every thousand million of sea-

This microphotograph of phytoplankton (the sea's floating plant life), which is a basic biological building-block, indicates the complexity of even the simplest organisms. No wonder the phytoplankton is vulnerable to such a pesticide as DDT, even a minute quantity of which impairs its ability to absorb sunlight and provide food for larger marine creatures.

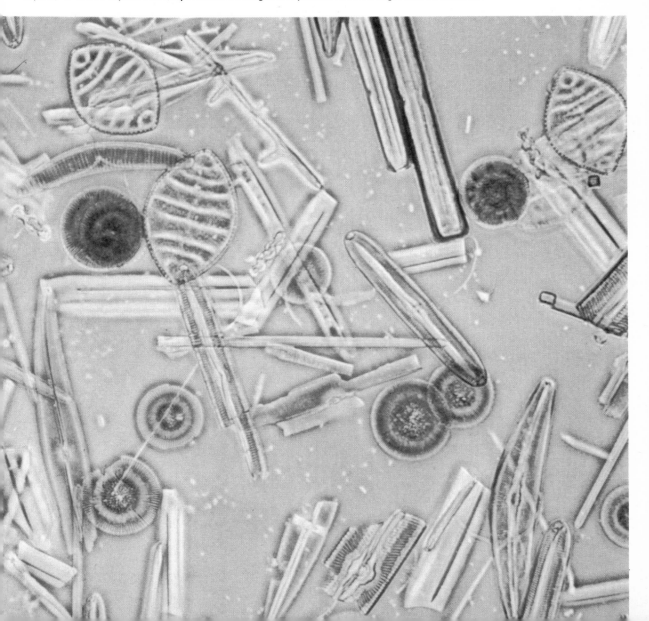

water. Marine phytoplankton—the microscopic floating plants that comprise the basic diet of many ocean creatures—live and grow by means of their ability to use the sun's energy for manufacturing their own food. DDT, it has been proved, interferes with this process of photosynthesis, and can therefore threaten all the different forms of life in the sea.

Nor is this merely a short-term danger, easy to overcome at an acute stage by banning a given pesticide. Many pesticides are extraordinarily persistent. More than one third of the amount of DDT sprayed on soil has been found to remain there for as much as 17 years. Similarly long-lived are such other major chemical pesticides as benzene, hexachloride, dieldrin, endrin, and aldrin (the so-called chlorinated hydrocarbons), and parathion, Malathion, Azodrin, and phosdrin (which are organophosphates, chemically related to nerve gases). All we have learned about the various pest-killers so far leads us to believe that they have far-reaching effects not only on pests but on the entire biosystem, and many biologists are convinced that they jeopardize the life-support processes of our planet.

One reason why we may have made so many careless mistakes in handling these dangerous substances is that we still know comparatively little about the soil itself. The soil is a complex ecosystem in its own right, with a numerous and very varied animal and organic population. One count, taken in a North Carolina forest, indicates that about 125 million small invertebrates (creatures without bones) are likely to inhabit a single acre of soil. And along with these mites, worms, and insects, there are millions upon millions of bacteria and microscopic plants—fungi, yeasts, algae, and suchlike—all of which play a part in the elaborate process of keeping the soil fertile and supporting life on top of it. These interconnected systems are all at risk from the chlorinated hydrocarbons and organophosphates, but how and to what extent we are still only beginning to learn.

We know even less about herbicides and their effects on the environment, and this is particularly unfortunate, because we use far more herbicide than insecticide. Two basic types are employed. The first, which includes herbicides mainly known by number (2,4-D; 2,4,5-T), causes plants to die by stimulating their metabolism; they literally grow themselves to death. Weed-killers of the second group, including

Above: the red admiral butterfly is a rare sight these days, because the nettles on which its larvae feed have dwindled in number as a result of crop and garden spraying. As the butterflies become fewer, the insects on which they used to prey prosper.

Right: the chrysanthemum is not only a lovely flower but the source of an excellent nonpolluting insecticide, pyrethrum. One probable reason why it is not more widely used is that the industrially produced pesticides are far more effectively advertised.

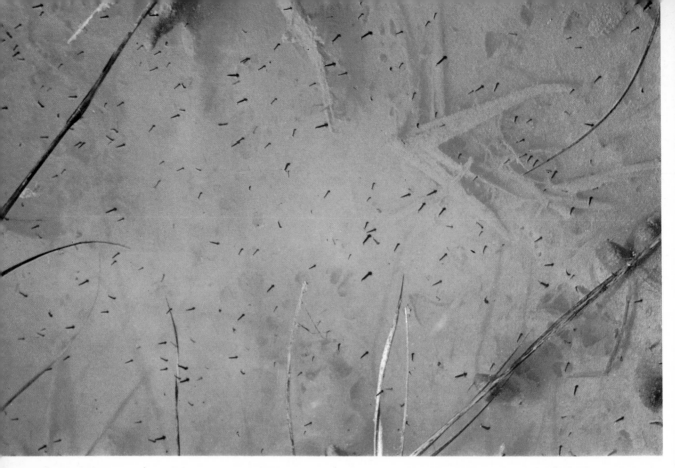

Removed from natural enemies, mosquitoes will breed in colossal numbers (the larvae are shown here in a marsh pond), and as transmitters of disease in warm climates they can become a health hazard. To treat the problem with DDT and similar chemicals, however, is to create other problems; the best method of control is to bring their natural enemies into mosquito territory.

simazine and diuron, block a crucial step in photosynthesis, causing the treated plant to starve to death. Although animals appear to be organically unaffected by the herbicides, their environments—and thus their survival patterns—are changed. When nettles have been sprayed, for example, the butterflies that breed on them vanish. You may look upon butterflies as simply a pleasing sight on a summer day, but they may be much more important to us than just that.

What, then, can we do to stop taking chances with our future? We could step up our efforts to find less dangerous alternatives to the chemical herbicides and insecticides now in use. There are already plenty of pesticides far less damaging to the environment than the organophosphates and chlorinated hydrocarbons. Some may be more expensive now, but this will not always be so, especially if the price of oil—a major factor because oil is an important ingredient of chemical pesticides—continues to rise. Governments that now subsidize compounds such as DDT could encourage the use of more desirable insecticides

such as carbamates or the botanical substances pyrethrum and rotenone, obtained from chrysanthemums and the roots of derris plants respectively. Such natural products are highly effective, yet much less ecologically harmful than the artificial chemicals. The reason why they are not being widely used is simply that they are not promoted, being of little profit to the agricultural chemicals industry. Just as importantly, governments do not subsidize their use, and therefore they are not forcefully marketed.

Perhaps the best possible alternative, however, would be for us to shift to a system of agriculture in which control and organization would replace attempts at wholesale extermination of pests. For example, mosquitoes can be reduced in number (something that no chemical has successfully accomplished) by draining the swamps in which they breed and by stocking adjacent lakes with mosquito-eating fish. In somewhat similar fashion, other appropriate predators and parasites can be matched against pests. Or the male of a given species can be neutered, as was done

Most insect pests can be controlled by nontoxic methods. Cater-pillars of the cinnabar moth (top) have been introduced into pastures afflicted with ragwort as a means of biological control of this pest weed. The paper wasp (center) feeds on the destructive tobacco hornworm, forming an attractive alternative to the use of chemical poisons. And the aphid population on green plants and fruit trees can be kept down by the introduction of the lace-wing (above), whose larvae feed on aphids.

with the cotton-eating screwworm in Peru after all chemical efforts had failed. Such methods of pest control could achieve the desired aims without the disastrous consequences of chemical "warfare," although it should be stressed that not all such biological controls are cure-alls.

As for alternatives to chemical fertilizers, the problems are urgent and require attention at the highest possible level, for only governments have the power to do what is needed. As we have seen, inorganic fertilizers generate the need for more and larger doses all the time. The risk is that the land itself will become progressively less fertile and that this will precipitate a food crisis. In addition, the nitrates and phosphates applied to the land will increasingly pollute our waters and overstrain our sewerage facilities.

It is an ironical fact that we are contaminating the waters of our rivers and streams not merely with these salts but also with farm and domestic manure, which could actually provide an alternative to chemical fertilizers, but which farmers are now treating as a waste product. To collect and distribute manure instead of throwing it away would pose some formidable organizational problems, but they are not insurmountable; nor need they cost large sums of money. At any rate, some biologists feel that no cost would be too great for any program that would return manure to the land and help to reconstruct the soil and to strengthen its organic content.

Hand in hand with such a program would go schemes for increasing the natural concentration of nitrates in the soil. One way to do this would be to grow more plants that actively encourage those microorganisms necessary for the conversion of nitrogen into organic nitrates. These microorganisms are often also responsible for the production of usable phosphorus and sulfur. Root plants in particular harbor them, and so we should do well to return to an emphasis on root and leguminous crops.

Indeed, we ought to be contemplating a farming way of life that would be both simpler—in its traditional union of men, animals, and plants—and more reliant on the complexity and variety of the natural environment. In changing our basic attitudes toward agriculture, we should need to abandon the technique of turning our farms into monocultural prairies, and we should have to return to a mixed high-yield organic system in which there was continuous recycling and "time off" for the soil to rehabilitate itself.

That way, there would be a new beginning to the fallowing that we should never have stopped.

It *can* be done. The turnabout is already happening in a small way in many parts of America and Europe. A very small but increasing minority of amateur farmers are joining the grow-it-yourself movement and finding that it not only saves substantial sums of money but also results in foods that are far tastier than those purchased through the conventional farm-packer-shop channels. One thing that such small-scale agriculturists can be certain of, is that the produce they grow will not be polluted if they habitually use purely organic techniques, composting and leaf-molding the soil and controlling pests with simple nonpersistent substances. Their methods are obviously not going to replace large-scale farming, but what they are doing is an important indication of some people's concern for a clean food environment.

Critics of the big-business approach to farming, in which machines and chemicals replace animals and men, are now beginning to attract attention in official quarters (an American government official talking about the energy crisis was moved to confess, in 1975, that the United States puts more chemical fertilizers on its lawns and golf courses than India spreads on its farmland). Originally rejected as eccentric and stupid, the critics have at least convinced entrenched authority that they are not asking for the overnight abolition of fertilizers and pesticides, but only for the gradual withdrawal of persistent chemicals and their replacement by biological and cultural controls. Some governments are listening and taking action, as are a good many rather bewildered farmers who know, instinctively or by the evidence in their own fields, that their efforts to increase efficiency over the last 30 years seem to have been misdirected.

It would be naive to expect a swift or unanimous agreement from governments, industry, and the farmers to return to earlier practices. Before they could do so, we should need to work out what to do with the enormous agrochemical industry that has grown up around the world. We should also need to reappraise many of the government subsidies that are now being paid. And we should have to look at the possibility of replacing machines with men in the fields—by no means an easy thing to do. Take the case of Britain, a small country that has lost one million men and as many horses from the land since the end of World War I and with an agrochemical industry that turns over $800 millions a year. The former field workers and their families are in the cities, many helping to manufacture tractors, combines, ditch-diggers, and agricultural chemicals. You cannot easily reverse a situation like that—and it would be even more difficult in larger countries such as West Germany, the United States, and Canada.

Of one fact, however, there seems little doubt: we *could* grow enough food and other agricultural products by old-fashioned means if we really wanted to. But it is unlikely that we can do it with the continuing use of intensive chemical control. And in the very process of failing in that job, we seem doomed to disrupt and destroy much of the natural environment. On balance, we have not yet reached the point of no return; but we are not very far off.

These two pictures sum up the change that has overtaken agriculture. At the beginning of the 20th century, when the above farm laborers with their scythes were photographed in an English field, there were 2 million men and 1 million horses working the land in Britain. By the beginning of the 1970s there were only 1 million men, aided by as many tractors. Long before that time, the agricultural revolution had spread far afield; the new tractors at the left have just come off the assembly line in São Paulo, Brazil. In country after country, the story is the same: the men and women who used to tend the soil, spread manure on the fields, care for the stock, and repair the hedges, now work in the cities making tractors, artificial fertilizers and pesticides, intensive rearing units, and chainlink fencing.

Pollution and Industry

People are more aware of the pollution caused by industrial processes than of any other kind. This is partly because industry-generated filth is often more apparent than pollution from other sources, but also because industrial organizations have recently been subjected to an outstanding amount of criticism for contaminating the environment. Sadly, some of the largest firms have sometimes been their own worst enemies. They have either denied that they were responsible for pollution even when the evidence has been there for everyone to see, or else, admitting responsibility, have promised swift action—and have done nothing. Having said this, however, I must point out that industry, like agriculture, is only responding to the general demand for a higher material standard of living. And so, if products and profits continue to take priority over pollution control, the fault is a communal one.

A case that illustrates these issues is the tragic situation at Minamata Bay in Japan, which came dramatically to light back in 1953 but which still affects the local population. In the 1950s, Japan, like other industrialized countries, had a fast-expanding chemical industry, and one of its basic products (which was used for making plastic resins and essential compounds such as octanol and dioctyl phthalate) was a chemical called acetaldehyde. It was in great demand. Production trebled in eight years, and the town of Minamata prospered along with its thriving chemical plant. At that time, the standard method for producing acetaldehyde involved the use of mercuric sulfate as a catalyst, and the effluents from this process inside the Minamata plant were eventually allowed to flow down a canal into the bay.

What no one then knew—and what took nearly 10 years to establish—was that the mercuric sulfate was turning into a deadly compound, methyl mercury, and that hundreds of tons of this substance were accumulating in the waters of Minamata Bay and in the bodies of its fish. The first signs of trouble occurred in 1953, when local cats began to go berserk; some even killed themselves by plunging into the sea. Soon afterward, the effects of the poison appeared in people, and the early symptoms—paralyzed hands, dilated pupils—became a familiar sight. Then

If prosperity is synonymous with pollution then this view of Cape Town is an appropriate reminder that South Africa has one of the highest standards of living enjoyed by white people anywhere in the world, accompanied by a chronic air-pollution problem.

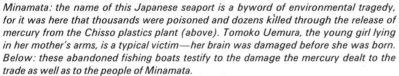

Minamata: the name of this Japanese seaport is a byword of environmental tragedy, for it was here that thousands were poisoned and dozens killed through the release of mercury from the Chisso plastics plant (above). Tomoko Uemura, the young girl lying in her mother's arms, is a typical victim—her brain was damaged before she was born. Below: these abandoned fishing boats testify to the damage the mercury dealt to the trade as well as to the people of Minamata.

severe cases of unexplained brain damage began to be recorded. It was the start of a virtual epidemic in which 45 people were to die and a further 70, many of them children, were to be permanently and horribly disabled. There is no known antidote to mercury poisoning.

At first, and for some years, the chemical plant admitted no liability for what was happening. Even when it became clear that the acetaldehyde process was producing an extremely toxic mercury effluent, the company continued to operate as before. And when lawsuits were filed, they were fought to the bitter end. Ultimately the company was forced to pay compensation to families of victims, to acknowledge its responsibility, and to mend its ways. But the effects of the

pollution lingered on. By the mid-1970s, some 500 cases of mercury poisoning in the bay area had been officially verified, and unofficial estimates put those still at risk in the 1000 to 10,000 range. The figures are hardly surprising because about 200,000 people used to eat fish from the contaminated waters of Minamata Bay.

Could a disaster on such a scale happen again? Could it happen in a country that is not expanding so hurriedly as Japan was in the 1950s? Would symptoms be picked up quickly, and would the causes be diagnosed promptly? Would companies and governments act responsibly if there were reasonable grounds for suspecting a particular industrial effluent of endangering the environment? Those are questions that we are all

in the human body can cause high blood pressure, cancer, cirrhosis, and brain damage.

Sometimes, however, the public knows full well what it is being exposed to but can find no satisfactory way to protect itself. Two of the most common industrial chemicals are ammonia and sulfuric acid; and wherever people live near works that make these essential chemicals, it has been traditionally accepted that curtains and other fabrics will be eaten away, eyes will be sore and runny, and paintwork will yellow and peel. In many such situations, those most affected rely for their livelihoods on the offending factories and are therefore reluctant to object. There are other places, though, where the pollution from acid and ammonia plants, together with the acids synthesized in the atmosphere from sulfur dioxide and water, affects such wide areas that effective protest is well-nigh impossible. The rain in parts of New Hampshire is now 100 times as acidic as it would be naturally; in Hawaii, tomato crops have been stunted by acidic rainwater; atmospheric acid in the Faroe Islands of the North Atlantic has begun to eat away at household paintwork. In each of those areas, the nearest center of industrial activity is hundreds or thousands of miles away!

Research into this question of the long reach of chemical pollution has undermined an earlier assumption that used to control abatement policy. That policy was based on the false belief that dispersion of smoke and chemical vapors from very tall chimneys—up to 800 feet high—would negate the effects. Further proof that this is not so has come from Sweden, which has formally protested to other European countries as a result of the 100-fold increase in its atmospheric acidity over the last 20 years. Most of the acidity, say the Swedes, comes from Britain, Germany, Poland, and the U.S.S.R.; and they blame it for a slow-down in local rates of forest growth, increased leaching of nutrients from farmland soil, and contamination of Sweden's lakes, which one study describes as having become "mild acid baths."

Hawaii, the Faroes, and Sweden are not yet suffering, of course, from the grim effects of

Drop by drop, oil and other petrochemical byproducts seep from the valves, joints, pumps, and pipes of a modern refinery. Constant vigilance is costly; to inspect every source of pollution would be a full-time job for an army of workers—which helps to explain the widespread failure to contain these types of pollution.

direct, outright toxicity. What threatens them (as well as the rest of us) is that they are being subjected to increasing quantities of pollutants that are perfectly bearable in small amounts. With a few exceptions, poisonous substances can be "lost" in the natural environment. Many of them will either degrade biologically or be physically absorbed out of harm's way. But sheer volume compounds the problem. The amount of sulfur dioxide being pumped into the air, for example, is already almost incomprehensibly large, but is growing faster than our rate of industrial production. Official predictions, agreed on by the United States, Japan, and most European nations, indicate that by 1980 the sulfur dioxide released into the atmosphere during that year will have jumped from less than 50 million tons in 1968 to 94 million tons. Separately, America has projected a doubling of this figure by the end of the century.

All over the world, local authorities are despairing of their ability to deal with growing quantities of industrial effluents. All over the world, antipollution laws are being outstripped or outdated by new manufacturing techniques and ever larger quantities of pollutants. And yet the pressure continues for more output, more products, and lower production costs.

Thus, although such irritants as hydrocarbon particles in smoke, oil spills, or even sulfuric acid are not in themselves persistent, their output is becoming large enough to overwhelm the capacity of the biosphere to absorb them. It has still not dealt with many pollutants from bygone industries or superseded processes—such as the tars from 19th-century textile-treatment plants, the chromium from old-fashioned tannery wastes, or the pickling acids from former steelmaking and tinplating plants. Yet it is now expected to absorb much larger volumes of greater toxicity, and sometimes of vicious persistence. In the persistent class come the heavy metals: lead, cadmium, mercury, beryllium, selenium, and nickel, to name only a few. Though traces of some of these elements may be necessary for normal bodily functioning, the amounts now being ingested directly and indirectly by man are a cause for great concern. There is already enough evidence to prove that they are harmful, for cases of heavy-metal poisoning are numerous and mostly well documented.

What we do not know is the degree of risk to which all of us are now continuously exposed.

How much of what kinds of pollutant is in the air we breathe today? How much in the water we drink? The seas? The soil? How much more will industry be adding tomorrow? These are questions to which we can give no accurate answers.

The variety and complexity of modern science and technology as applied to the demands of society make it more and more difficult to assess risk, prevent environmental accidents, and find causes or cures. As I write, 60 men and women in southern England have been rushed to the hospital after exposure to a leakage of ethylene oxide at a chemical plant. None of them seems likely to be permanently harmed by the gas—which is an ingredient in the manufacture of

Coal mining has always had an environmentally poor image: pitheads scarring the landscape, roads and rail sidings littered with coal and debris, and derelict buildings. The pithead above is typical of a scene that has changed little in 100 years, and the miners on the left, though greatly assisted in their labor by modern machinery, are still exposed to unique kinds of danger and disease. A particularly prevalent menace is pneumoconiosis, a virtually incurable bronchial affliction caused by the inhalation of coal dust.

Right: waste material from coal mines is generally dumped in enormous heaps nearby, marring the visual environment, sterilizing the land beneath, and often catching fire in a process of spontaneous combustion and burning slowly for years. But this waste heap at Aberfan in Wales was responsible for disaster of a more tragic kind. In 1964, softened by rain and mine waters, it suddenly avalanched onto a school building and killed almost every child in the town. Despite this terrible event, similar waste heaps continue to exist.

surgical sutures—but the factory has admitted that many fatalities could easily have occurred as a result of the accident. "We shall not know for a considerable time why the leak took place," adds a company statement; "the machinery involved is so very complex."

There *are* people who would not class an in-the-factory release of toxic substances as "pollution." But why not? The effects are the same as if the victims had been 100 miles away. An unintentional or careless release of poisonous materials is no less disturbing because it happens inside an industrial plant instead of outside it. And this raises a further point: if a substance presents a direct, immediate risk to those handling it at a factory, may there not also be risks for those of us who are exposed to it later in one way or another?

An indication of the answer can be found in certain facts about polyvinyl chloride (familiarly

Until recently, it was believed that very tall chimneys, such as the power-station smokestack above, would disperse noxious vapors and particles without damage to the aerial environment. We now have conclusive proof that this is not so. Increasing concentrations of industrially produced chemicals have been detected in wildernesses and remote places all over the world. The area directly below a huge chimney may be uncontaminated by its effluents, but industry has a long environmental reach. In the Faroe Islands (right), out in the North Atlantic and hundreds of miles from the nearest factory, high acid levels in rain have begun to take their toll of paintwork, fabrics, and people's health.

known as PVC), an unusually popular plastic. It has been known for some time that people who work in plants where the raw vinyl chloride monomer gas is transformed into the plastic can contract liver disease as a result of the exposure. Now scientists in West Germany and the United States have found evidence of similar liver diseases in the thousands of workers involved in further processes in which polyvinyl chloride is molded, extruded, melted, or shaped into a variety of articles for daily use. When the scientists reported their findings to an especially convened meeting in New York, they told observers that the range of symptoms detected included enlarged livers, damaged spleens, blood changes, skin disorders, and also pathological changes in bones, lungs, and blood circulation.

Shortly afterward, the U.S. Department of Labor announced that releases of the raw monomer gas should be kept to a safe level of less than one part per million. But a director of Europe's largest chemical company commented that requirements like this "would bring the industry to a halt . . . and would bring other industries, including coal mining and the motor industry, to a halt as well." He was absolutely right; for a time, at least, the industry *would* grind to a halt. But we have not always had plastics, and the fact that polyvinyl is a supremely useful material must be weighed against the fact that its usefulness is bought by endangered health within and outside the industry. It is well to remember, too, that thousands of tons of domestic items made from this plastic are annually thrown away and burned as rubbish, thus adding to the pollution burden.

Another material that threatens the health of the public as well as of those who come in direct factory contact with it is asbestos. It has been processed on a commercial scale for nearly a

Above: liquid and solid wastes from every part of Britain are dumped at this site on the Thames estuary. For 20 years chemical companies and others have dumped up to 50 million tons of toxic waste here each year, causing great public concern.

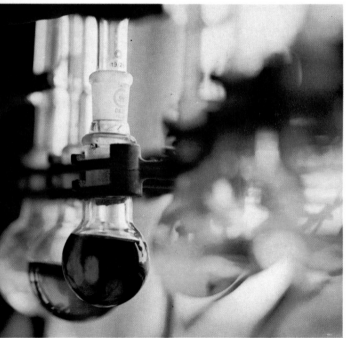

Above: chemical wastes are tested to see if they are suitable for incineration. Unfortunately, in real life the scale is much larger, and there are people around. Right: chemical waste that has traveled through densely populated areas by road is pumped into storage tanks to await disposal by burning.

century and is used for such innocent purposes as insulating pipes and lining ironing boards. Its most common application has been in vehicle braking systems; the fact that every train, car, truck, and plane contains asbestos accounts for its meteoric rise in consumption from a total worldwide production of 30,000 tons in 1910 to well over 4 million tons a year in the 1970s. Yet we have known since the earliest years of the asbestos industry that this was not a harmless material. Back in the 1890s, during the first five years' working of an asbestos mill in France, 50 workers died of a disease that postmortem examinations established as in some way connected with the fibrous materials that they were working with. In the early 20th century, asbestos dust was clearly identified as the deadly agent of what is commonly called *asbestosis*—a cancerous condition that has become more and more prevalent not only among workers in the industry, but among people who are merely in contact with the manufactured material.

Homeowners who use asbestos cement, builders who saw asbestos wallboard, operators of brake-testing machines—such people swell the list of victims. Asbestosis is a cancer of the membrane that surrounds the lung and the inner body cavity, and it is incurable. For nearly 50 years it has been recognized as a public hazard, not just an occupational risk. The average car, for

instance, wears out four sets of brake linings and two clutch linings during its service life. The wearing-out process creates asbestos particles, which are distributed in the environment to be inhaled by all of us. One eminent pathologist has estimated that asbestos dust will soon rival cigarettes as a cause of lung cancer. Even so, we continue to use it widely and thoughtlessly. Soft drinks are filtered through it. Surgeons use asbestos powder to speed up the healing of wounds. Children are given it, mixed with water, to use as a plaything. And a teaspoonful is more than enough to kill. Once asbestosis strikes, the victim may take as much as 20 years to die, but death from the disease is certain. We have known all this for a long time, but we have still done comparatively little to prevent it.

Potentially, though, the most hazardous of all substances is plutonium, the artificial radioactive element that is produced when uranium has been used in a nuclear reactor. Plutonium, which is itself a fuel for more advanced reactors, is the most poisonous substance known to man. A piece the size of an orange contains enough cancer-causing material to afflict everyone on earth with leukemia. One thousandth of a gram— you couldn't even see it on the point of a pin—is enough to kill a man. And yet nuclear plants are dealing with it in 5- to 15-ton quantities, and have been doing so for years. Only now are some of the risks becoming fully understood. In America and Britain, both of which have advanced nuclear-power programs, there is increasing anxiety not only about nuclear workers' safety but about the exposure of the general public to radiation emitted by plutonium wastes.

Among workers who handle plutonium, the chance of contracting cancer of the bone marrow is now thought to be at least 20 times greater than for anyone outside the industry. This is in spite of what appear to be stringent precautions inside each plant, where workers in active areas are daily monitored and removed from those areas if their radiation dosage exceeds a maximum level for the day. Many eminent scientists now feel that there is *no* safe maximum, that *any* exposure is unacceptable. These same authorities are expressing concern about radioactive wastes, which must be kept away from living environments for hundreds—some for thousands—of years. The problem of making the wastes secure is far from solved. In the short term, they can be stored in relative safety (barring sabotage or

Polyvinyl chloride is a harmless plastic that is fashioned into such useful things as these baskets in a Brazilian market. But the gas from which it is made is so dangerous that U.S. officials warn against exposing factory workers to air containing more than one part in a million. Even that much is risky; some countries advocate a manufacturing ban until safe production techniques are developed.

theft). In the long term, we are putting at risk generations unborn and cultures unknown. Modern man has spared no effort to dig up the physical remains of his distant past. Can we not assume that, hundreds of years from now, our descendants will do the same—but with catastrophic results?

The plutonium dilemma throws into sharp relief our basic predicament: having developed an extraordinarily advanced technology, we run the risk of being battered by it; far from solving our problems (such as how to generate more electric power), it may well create new problems that we are unprepared to deal with. This is true of less advanced technologies, too, in particular of the extractive industries—mining and quarrying. Objections to these industries used to center around the fact that they were unbeautiful, and so they often were. No lover of the natural environment can be particularly pleased by the sight of vast open-pit and strip mines. But as the extractive industries have expanded—they are now doubling at least every

14 years—and as the techniques have advanced (many mining plants can now extract and process 30 tons a minute), concern has grown for the more practical effects of such operations.

The first effect of an extractive operation is to change the landscape dramatically and, for all practical purposes, irreversibly. A typical example is the world's largest copper mine at Bougainville in the Solomon Islands, where thick tropical jungle has been killed with herbicides and cleared by means of blasting and high-speed logging (drawing a steel hawser rapidly through the air between two powerful winches). The removal of vegetation has sizably increased the amount of water runoff from the land, and thus the rate of soil erosion. It must also have changed the local climate by removing wind cover, reducing photo-synthetic activity and oxygen exchange, and introducing innumerable particles into the air (for the vegetation has been burned in heaps, assisted by fuel oil and large fans). Finally, before the mining process was started, nearly 30 million tons of soft topsoil were washed away

The main effluent from fission reactions decays to half its original strength in 30 years. The waste also contains tiny traces of unrecovered plutonium, which takes 24,000 years to decay to half of its original strength. At present the waste is stored in cooled tanks like this one (cost about $2,500,000), but a plant is to be built to turn the waste into an easily stored solid, glass-like substance.

This aerial view of a copper mine near Great Salt Lake, Utah, gives some idea of the vast scale on which extractive industries operate. Capable of mining and processing up to 30 tons of material a minute, such a pit does lasting damage to a far wider area than just the site itself, and the damage, seldom repaired by industry after it has taken what it wants from the earth, will last for many decades.

with water jets from 725-horsepower pumps, and then bulldozed into a nearby mountain river.

During the mining operations that are now going on, exposed copper ores release their salts into the watershed in an accelerating and concentrated process. Together with the inevitable pollutants from any such plant—lime, fuel oil, lubricating oils, metal-bearing dusts, and sewage—the effect has been to disrupt soil, wildlife, farming, fishing, and humanity in general within an area of more than 100 square miles. Nor will things return to their earlier state if and when mining operations cease. In one Welsh estuary, for example, a recent attempt to hatch oysters failed because of the runoff from some small and long-abandoned lead and zinc workings.

Drilling for oil is, of course, the newest extractive industry, and it may turn out to be one of the worst offenders. Anyone who has seen an oilfield, with its associated plant and machinery, will know what it does to the environment. What *might* be done in our age of accident and sabotage is horrible to contemplate. Even normal operating conditions make a harsh assault on natural surroundings, with oil seepage, plant scrap, flare smoke, and vehicular congestion. Any major failure, such as the collapse of a rig, the rupture of a pipeline, the collision of tankers, or the firing of a tank farm (all of which have happened in recent years), brings about a massive environmental degradation from which recovery is unlikely for centuries. The beaches and flatlands of the world's main oil-producing regions testify to the impact that drilling has on the surrounding earth and its waters. That impact is being enormously intensified with each new day.

To what extent, then, can naturally self-purifying systems, such as rivers, be safely used as dumping grounds for industrial effluents? The answer must be that we are already demanding too much of them. The importance of rivers and natural ecosystems to our survival can hardly be overstated, for they help to ensure breathable air, fertile farmland, and edible fish. What can we do?

One thing we can do is to stand back and assess whether the damage to the environment that industry perpetrates is the inherent fault of a given technology or whether it arises from the *misuse* of that technology. If the technology itself is the culprit (as seems to be the case, for instance, in some aspects of nuclear fission), only the most dedicated kind of research can be expected to find answers to the problem. But a great deal of industrial pollution can be attributed to carelessness. Smoking chimneys, millions of gallons of heated water discharged from power stations and factory boilers, oils and chemicals draining away from refineries and process plants— these all represent waste on a colossal scale, a scale that is becoming physically and economically less and less tenable. Industrialists and governments alike, therefore, have been forced to begin evolving ways of avoiding this waste; and the trend will undoubtedly speed up as our use of land intensifies, for virtually no one today can escape the effects of industrial pollution.

Even if a captain of industry were so short-sighted as to want to break antipollution laws, self-interest and the power of public relations would teach him a lesson. Nobody can live so far from his plant and its neighboring plants that he remains unaware of any environmental disruption they may cause. The modern industrialist is likely to know whether his factory is releasing contaminants into the air because he is able to see them and will be told—in no uncertain terms— by protesting members of the public. If he complains about the price of water, he soon learns how much it costs either to remove industrial effluent from the drinking supplies, or to bring in unpolluted water from upstream.

Out of a growing recognition of the need for reform has sprung a new, or relatively new, profession: technology assessment. Technology assessors weigh the advantages of various industrial developments against the social and environmental costs. What are the gains, and what are the losses? These are the simple criteria behind each examination. The ultimate assessment, however, is a lot less simple to make. How, for instance, can we weigh the gains in transport efficiency of some types of aircraft against the undoubted loss of environmental stability for people living near airports?

One interesting—though perhaps not very scientific—way to do this is to ask the people themselves. Three or four years ago, residents near London's Heathrow Airport were asked how much they would willingly pay to be rid of the aerial pollution, including noise, caused by a proposed jetliner, which had been tested along a flightpath over their homes. The total of their hypothetical payments exceeded the sum of the calculated profit to the airline company of running that aircraft and the estimated savings for businessmen using it in preference to a

Above: when the Torrey Canyon, *a supertanker, went aground off the southwest coast of Britain in 1967, hundreds of miles of beach in Britain and France were contaminated and much marine life was killed by oil spillage. To get rid of the oil that remained in the wreck, the Royal Air Force set it on fire by dropping bombs, thus releasing pollution into the air instead of the sea. Although the most dramatic marine oil spill so far, it was not the worst.*

The Rio Tinto, as its name indicates, has always been stained with the salts of copper, which is widely deposited in this region of southwestern Spain. But never was the river as appallingly contaminated as it has been since large-scale extraction and processing of the ores got under way, a few years ago. Not surprisingly, it can now support no life at all.

Who benefits and who loses out when advanced technology is given its head? For a majority of the world's people, modern aircraft such as the Boeing 747s parked at London's Heathrow airport are a source only of noise pollution and a reminder that the earth's resources are unequally shared. But it is increasingly accepted that vehicles like these are highly inefficient in that they consume more energy than the results warrant. In fact, the tide of informed opinion seems to be turning against high-technology, high-cost transport. It is significant that the supersonic Anglo-French Concorde, seen below at Toulouse, has failed to arouse much enthusiasm. Environmental objections to its use have been voiced in practically every major country where it might operate.

smaller, slower plane. Although the argument did not win the day at that particular moment in history, it might carry considerably more weight if advanced today or tomorrow.

Other profit-and-loss assessments, based more realistically on facts and figures rather than opinion, are being listened to by more and more people within the industrialized nations. Essentially, such assessments involve two basic standards: human health and the productivity of the land. Both can be measured in coldly effective terms of cost. In a world where every highly industrialized country is trying desperately to

in manufacturing environmentally intolerable products or operating ecologically questionable plants. Manufacturers must remain reasonably free to innovate and develop. Informed governments must have the right to resist objections and challenge environmental protest. But all must be kept keenly aware of pollution; and decisions about jobs, product development, and environmental laws must be made openly and must be firmly grounded on impartial data.

You may see this as an impossible ideal. I grant that it is a very difficult one, but it is not impossible. Even now, several major industries in Europe, America, and Japan are rethinking the methods they established and took for granted only a decade ago. Materials are being used with greater care, and reused wherever possible. To some extent, no doubt, this has been dictated primarily by a new need for economizing, but that is no bad thing. If the best way to emphasize the evils of waste and pollution is through the wallet, so be it; the end result will be just as beneficial as if reform were originated for ethical and altruistic concern. Economics and ecological morality are, in any case, directly linked. The more we pollute our environment, the more we shall have to spend to clean it up. The more efficiently we recycle materials, the less we shall have to lay out in municipal disposal costs.

The real goal, as far as industry is concerned, is to make as much use as we can of the technologies developed over the past two centuries without destroying the environment. No sensible critic of the current state of affairs would insist that we must go backward. It is, rather, our duty to question each so-called "advance," to define the word "progress." Should a given job be done by a machine rather than a man? If his job is taken from him, what will the man be doing instead—making the machine? What effect will that have environmentally? Is such and such a product one that positively must be made from plastics? Again, why and at what costs?

To ask such questions is to face up to fundamental issues. And because it is the ordinary individual's demands and choices that ultimately determine what industry decides to make (or not to make), the chief responsibility for what happens from now on rests in the ordinary individual's hands. So the best place to look for answers is probably within our own four walls. What are we doing in our homes to encourage or to combat pollution?

cut such imports as fertilizers, other agricultural chemicals, and raw materials for farm machinery, and where there is a strong determination to reduce the social and monetary costs of illness, the comparisons are beginning to show.

Without a degree of social upheaval that would be unacceptable to most of us, the reforms necessary for reducing the environmental impact of industry have to be fairly gentle, of course. Only as part of a planned program for the care and maintenance of our society as well as our planet can they be made to work. Jobs cannot be swept away overnight because the workers are engaged

then they have become widely available; finally, they have come to seem indispensable. The only thing that has changed since the late 18th century is that the process has been immensely speeded up. Thus, canned food took a century to pass from the inventor's workshop to the mass market; the motor car took 30 years; the television receiver, 10; the pocket calculator, 5; the portable video camera, 3.

What we have to ask is whether the mere availability of a product must always lead to its being wanted—and, only too often, wasted. The answer is not easy, but it does seem that each of the above inventions (like many others) has actively changed our society in a way that has made it become necessary. The automobile is the best example. It has brought about social and physical changes that in themselves force us to have automobiles; shops, places of employment, homes, leisure centers, and schools are no longer clustered together, precisely because it is correctly assumed that most of those using these facilities have access to cars. And because public transport is used less and less, it becomes less and less

Labor-saving appliances pour through showrooms like this one by the million. But whose labor is being saved, and what are the environmental consequences of using mechanized aids in the home? In each case there is a pollution cost to be counted.

available. So it is that the availability of cars has indeed made them indispensable.

That it *is* possible to change the situation and to become less enslaved by wasteful imaginary "needs" was proved in the early 1970s. Faced with a shortage of cheap energy, many people learned that, when waste or careless use of energy became expensive, they could quickly adapt to using less, often without significantly altering their standard of living. So we can still learn to share our cars more, to insulate our homes against heat loss, to cut out unnecessary journeys, to try to make household articles last longer, and so on. We might do it initially in order to save money, but the wider impact would be felt in energy conservation, and we should thus be avoiding some of the pollution we cause. Where savings become more difficult to bring about, however, is where there is a conflict between what we can, and perhaps should, do on an individual basis and what we allow to be done on our behalf. Take garbage and sewage, for instance. From family to family, we may cut down on the volume of liquid and solid wastes that are

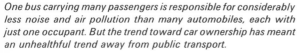
One bus carrying many passengers is responsible for considerably less noise and air pollution than many automobiles, each with just one occupant. But the trend toward car ownership has meant an unhealthful trend away from public transport.

discharged from our homes, but there are still enormous quantities left to dispose of. What are we to do about them?

Few municipal problems are more pressing than the question of the disposal of the huge quantities of garbage and sewage. Yet it must be disposed of. How to do this without further harm to the environment is a matter of enormous concern to everyone, and local authorities are constantly searching for new and better disposal methods. Various schemes for burning solid wastes and using the resultant heat as a source of power, or for extracting gas and oil from household rubbish, have been put forward; but none so far has proved really feasible, because collection and distribution of waste for such purposes is too

costly for the amount of energy that could actually be recovered. And so the best answer to the problem remains the simplest—and the most difficult: instead of a widespread municipal attempt to recover materials, we must in the first place teach every family to avoid scrapping anything that is still usable.

One practical way to "teach" domestic economy of this sort is, as I have already indicated, through the purse. People are less likely to litter the countryside with empty cans and bottles if they are forced to pay for the privilege. Thus, the state of Oregon has made nonreturnable bottles illegal. When the law was first passed, one of the major soft-drink companies protested that to require a purchaser to pay a high deposit on a bottle of soft drink and to forfeit the money on any unreturned bottle would reduce sales. But it did no such thing. It did reduce the amount of broken glass in Oregon's fields and roads, however, and the company itself has now introduced

Domestic waste from one week in one street (left); and from one day in one corner of a city park (below). There would be far less if we were all forced to pay directly the environmental costs of creating each item of litter. As it is, we make eyesores of our wastes and let them pollute the air and soil.

similar programs in several other places (though initially, it must be said, only where a temporary shortage of glass threatens supplies).

All over the world, indeed, the returnable bottle and the reusable container show signs of making a comeback. Not long ago, for example, French vintners decided to abandon the plastic containers in which they had been bottling *vin ordinaire* and to return to reusable glass. One of their reasons was entirely economic: the plastic bottles were costing too much. But other considerations also led to the decision. For one thing, there was the risk to workers handling vinyl chloride monomer, the dangerous raw material from which the plastic was made. And, secondly, many French towns were expressing concern at the build-up of plastic refuse. In effect, the vintners took a community-minded approach to the problem that confronted them.

Inevitably, though, many people resist pressures to economize whenever economies seem "inconvenient." Modern man is used to buying what he wants and throwing away whatever he has no further need for. As he tosses his cans and bottles out of the car, he does not concern himself with the problem of pollution. Nor does his wife as she fills her cupboards with sheets, shirts, and stockings made of synthetic materials. Nylon, wear-resistant plastics, and other synthetics are all nondegradable, of course. Everyone knows that there is very little you can do with discarded items made from these materials other than burn them, which releases toxic gases into the air, or bury them in the ground, where they will remain intact or become unearthed and litter the landscape. A neighbor of mine has just added a pile of worn-out cotton garments to his compost heap, delighted in the knowledge that the cotton will enrich and freshen the soil. But how many of the rest of us are buying, wearing, and discarding natural fibers these days?

It is no doubt true that an economic argument

Contrasting street scenes of yesterday and today. An old-fashioned hardware store was a positive riot of goods, most of which are nearly impossible to find in our throwaway age. Galvanized and enameled buckets and trashcans, wooden curtain rods, assorted screws and nails sold by the pound, and many miscellaneous items (with very little surplus packaging in evidence) add up to a strikingly different sight from the view on the sidewalk of a modern American Main Street. The products of America's giant soft-drinks industry now cover the face of the globe. But we pay for the convenience of their dispensable packing by having to look at the disowned and wasteful ugliness of today's city streets.

in favor of modern wash-and-wear fabrics is that they last longer than do cotton and silk. But this is a case where the saving of money in the short run can lead to vastly expensive environmental degradation in the long run. And for uses other than clothing, the synthetic material is often much less durable—in a useful state, that is—than the natural ones that it has superseded.

Take, for instance, the enameled or galvanized steel utensils that were sold widely in the first half of this century. It was not uncommon for such buckets, washbowls, garbage cans, and so forth to last for 10 or more years. And when, having deteriorated beyond the point of repair, they were scrapped, they could either be reclaimed as feedstock for new iron and steel or would rust innocently away in earth dumps. They have now been largely replaced by articles made from polypropylene and other so-called thermoplastics, which have a much shorter working life, tend to split or tear in ways that do not lend themselves to repair, and cannot practicably be recovered for secondary use.

In an effort to diminish our modern mountains of litter, some authorities have promoted the idea of manufacturing decomposable plastics— ones that are constructed in such a way as to accelerate their normally slow aging and decomposing properties. Again, though, the theory may be all right, but it does not work in practice. First of all, decomposable plastics are unrealistically expensive to produce. And a second, more important disadvantage is that such plastics do not just dissolve into thin air: when they decompose, they pollute soil and ground water.

What we ought to be doing, then, is looking for ways to use fewer materials that pollute the environment, and trying to return to more traditional methods and materials. To what extent we can achieve this depends largely on whether we can bring about changes in the Western family's life style without making the changes too painful. Before there can be drastic physical changes, there must be a change of attitudes, an informed willingness to learn to do without some of the more obviously wasteful modern conveniences. In both America and Western Europe, groups of mainly (but not invariably) young people are already adopting a style of life based on this principle of foresighted rejection of extravagance. The whole concept of self-sufficiency is embraced by what they are doing; whether singly or in groups, they are growing their own food, re-

cycling their wastes, and making as little use as possible of manufactured products.

The key phrase there is "as little use as possible." I have visited houses built since 1970 where I could find no trace of anything that came from a factory, where the deliberate policy of the inhabitants has been to make absolutely everything from scratch, to turn all sewage into fertilizer and methane gas (for cooking), to grow all food by organic means, and to till the land with implements carved from natural wood. But not many households like this are likely to flourish. To begin with, most people today lack the expertise and the experience to live self-sufficiently. Very few could even construct a simple forest bivouac, let alone discover the correct mix for natural fertilizer. Moreover, there would have to be a radical redistribution of land in order to provide space for more than a few people to live like this, even if they restricted themselves to a vegetarian diet.

Still, such attempts at the simple life are not a waste of time. Like expensive government projects for building so-called "eco-houses," which generate power from wind-machines, solar panels, and waterwheels, and which make extensive use of sophisticated equipment for regulating temperatures and so on, they can at least give a few good ideas to ordinary citizens living in ordinary 20th-century houses. Thus, it is eminently possible for people to conserve energy by not conspicuously throwing it away, to make use of devices such as solar generators if it is proved that they are locally more energy- and cost-effective, and to conduct their domestic lives as if every material they used were precious. One very important lesson that the advocates of self-sufficiency can teach us is that we should probably stop thinking in terms of the "convenience" of living in the city. We should, indeed, reappraise the existing environmental situation very carefully before we encourage any further concentration of people in urban centers.

On the face of it, you might think that a great mass of people living close together could, by sharing their pollution problems, reduce the overall load. It does not work that way in practice, though. A number of problems interact, and the first and most important of these is lack of space. In New York, Tokyo, and London, three of the most densely populated cities of the developed countries, there is no land at all to spare. Particularly in the inner areas of such

Packaging and the Environment

	Paper					**Plastics**
	Wrapping paper, paper bags	Cardboard boxes, cartons	Wax paper	Cellophane and cellulose	Plastic-coated paper	Polythene bottle bags and fi…
Use	Millions of paper bags are used every day in shops.	Mostly used for outer packaging.	For wrapping sandwiches and similar uses.	Often used with cardboard in order to view contents. Also for candy wrappers.	Same as paper and board.	Most widely use… plastic for pack… aging. There is a… increasing use… "shrink" wrappin… for some goods.
Disposal Litter	Many paper bags and wrapping end up as litter. They decompose in time.	Decomposes in time.	Less easily degraded than other papers.	Same as other papers.	Plastic does not decompose.	Does not degrade… It is often bright color and easi… blown about. An… mals may choke o… it and small childre… may suffocate.
Controlled dumping	Easily compacted and eventually degrades. Low density. Blows about in high winds.	Same as other papers.	Same as other papers.	Same as other papers.	Same as other paper products, except it does not readily decompose.	Gets blown abou… even when we… Resistant to chem… cal and biologic… degradation.
Incineration	Good material for incineration. Volume of refuse decreased considerably when paper is burned.	Same as other papers.	Same as other papers.	Same as other papers.	Same as other papers.	Same as paper. N… toxic fumes whe… burned. When me… ted may clog inci… erator grates.
Pulverization	Easily pulverized.	Same as other papers.	Same as other papers.	Same as other papers.	Same as other papers.	No problem.
Composting	Biodegradable, but takes longer than vegetable matter.	Same as other papers.	Same as other papers, but less easily degradable.	Completely biodegradable in time.	Plastic residue left in compost when paper decomposes.	Not degradable b… inert.
Degradability	Completely biodegradable in time.	Same as other papers.	Same as other papers.	Completely biodegradable in time.	Plastic is not degradable and also inhibits the degradation of the paper.	Plastics in commo… use are not y… degradable.
Reclamation Reuse	Only possible in some cases. Brown paper wrapping can often be used several times.	Can be reused if not damaged.	Can be reused.	Reuse not feasible.	Unlikely to be reused.	Some plastic co… tainers can be use… many times.
Recycling	Most fibers could be recovered and recycled if it were economic to do so.	More uniform and more easily recoverable than wrapping paper.	Cannot easily be reclaimed.	Not reclaimable after use.	Not recoverable. Causes problems when recycling other paper, and results in impurity in finished product.	Mixed plasti… packaging wast… can be recycled. A… present plastics a… not recoverab… from househo… wastes.

An idea of how complex our pollution problem has become can be gained from this simplified chart showing various packaging materials and their impact on the natural environment. Even before we consider how to dispose of the vast quantities of waste and litter, we should stop to think of the energy-consuming and polluting processes involved in manufacturing the packaging sub-

		Cloth/Wood	**Metals**			**Glass**
...panded ...lystyrene	Polyvinyl chloride (PVC)	Sacks, boxes	Tinned steel and plain steel cans	Aluminum cans and foil	Aerosol cans	Containers, bottles
...d mostly for ...kaging delicate ...gs such as ...os or fruit.	Used for coating paper and in various containers.	Sacks, string, wooden cases, and boxes.	Tin cans mostly used for food packaging.	Nonreturnable aluminum cans are used for various drinks. Kitchen foil is widespread, as well as foil for milk bottles, etc.	Used for hair sprays, insect sprays, etc.	Returnable bottles are used for some soft drinks, beer, and milk. Nonreturnable containers are used for almost everything else.
...ne as polythene. ...y light and more ...ily blown about.	Same as polythene.	Sacks and boxes do not add much to the general litter problem.	Do not degrade quickly. Noisy when blown about.	Becoming a widespread litter problem. Aluminum does not degrade.	Unlikely to make much contribution to litter.	Drink bottles make up most of glass litter.
...ne as polythene.	Same as polythene.	Easily compacted and eventually degrades. High density.	Cause no problems.	Cause no problems. Aluminum does not degrade.	Not much of a problem — slight danger of explosion.	Cause no problems.
...ne as polythene ...does not melt.	Noxious fumes produced when incinerated.	Easily combustible.	Incineration only removes labels and food residues.	Cans usually unaffected.	Explode when heated.	Usually melt and mix with ash to form clinker.
...problem.	No problem.	No problem.	Broken into fist-size lumps, but cannot easily be baled.	No problem.	Explode when pulverized.	Easily pulverized.
...ne as polythene.	Same as polythene.	Same as paper.	No good for composting. Have to be removed.	No good for composting. Have to be removed.	No good for composting and explosion a hazard.	No good for composting. Have to be removed.
...ne as polythene.	Same as polythene.	Completely biodegradable although takes much longer than paper.	Will rust and eventually disintegrate into oxides.	Aluminum cans and foil do not degrade.	Same as steel cans except for plastic parts.	Not degradable but inert.
...t easily reused — ...i be shredded ...d used for insula-...n.	Same as polythene.	Sacks and boxes can be reused unless damaged.	Not reusable except for such things as rubbish bins if large enough.	Cooking foil can be reused several times if handled carefully.	Useless when finished and dangerous to tamper with.	Milk bottles, for example, may do 30 trips, but washing and sterilizing require energy and cause pollution.
...t reclaimable.	Same as polythene.	Not reclaimable at present except for large quantities of sacks. Wood can be used as a fuel.	Many thousands of tons are reclaimed each year, some of which go for detinning to reclaim tin.	Can be recycled but reclamation difficult unless separation occurs in the household.	Cannot easily be reclaimed.	Smashed glass can be used in glass manufacture. It can also be used for making abrasives.

stances in the first place. To take a simple example: every ton of paper we produce uses up 17 fully grown trees, 275 pounds of sulfur, 350 pounds of limestone, 60,000 gallons of water, 9000 pounds of steam, and 255 kilowatt-hours of electricity. Less than one tenth of this wealth of material is reclaimed in the form of salvaged paper, although this is one of the easiest of man's products to recycle.

Left: Alexander Pike is one of a new kind of architects who are keenly interested in building urban houses that are close to being energy self-sufficient. He is shown here with a model of the house he designed in a government-sponsored research project at Cambridge University, England. Like some other "autonomous" houses, Pike's would be practically independent of outside supplies, with a water recycler, a sewage processor, a solar heater, and a wind machine to generate additional electric power.

Even in the heart of big cities it is possible to grow a great deal of food. The Friends of the Earth have been given official permission by the Greater London Council to plant vegetable crops on derelict land in the city. Demand for small urban plots of land—provided free in British cities to residents who undertake to cultivate them—has never been higher. Growing one's own food is cheaper than buying it, and the amateur farmer can avoid polluting the land with chemicals.

metropolises, the daytime pressure on space is enormous: huge commuting populations, traffic congestion, building and construction works all combine to produce outsized waste and pollution problems. The result is stress—stress on human beings and municipal services alike.

Linked with the space problem is the impossibility of running efficient transportation facilities. Frustration piles on frustration as buses, subway trains, and private vehicles vie for the right of way. As city rents and taxes rise, municipal services lag for lack of money. Housing pressures accumulate, slums proliferate, and the law becomes harder to enforce, even in such relatively simple matters as parking rules, noise abatement, litter prevention, and smoke control. Is it any wonder that the city dweller, confronted by a permanent crisis of rising costs and falling environmental standards, reacts by fitting out his own home with every possible comfort-making gadget and appliance?

A few years ago, a United States Secretary of Transportation painted the bleak big-city picture in this way: "If someone were to tell you that he had seen strings of noxious gases drifting among the buildings of a city, black smoke blotting out the sun, great holes in the major streets filled with men in hard hats, planes circling overhead unable to land, and thousands of people in those streets, pushing and shoving in a desperate effort to get out of the city . . . you would be hard pressed to know whether he was talking about a city at peace or at war." He was talking about New York, but he could have been describing Paris, Berlin, London, or Tokyo. Rome pours untreated wastes into the river Tiber at the rate of 60 cubic yards a minute; Los Angeles doctors have been known to urge residents who have no compelling reason to remain to move away because of the city's chronic air-pollution levels; Hong Kong, where the population has multiplied sixfold since World War II, drains the whole of its effluent into the sea.

The most dramatic example of metropolitan pollution is probably that of Tokyo, which stands at the center of what has been until quite recently the world's fastest-growing industrial economy. Tokyo's waste-collection system embodies the ultimate mixture of all the problems we have been looking at. Garbage men noisily collect a total of nearly 15,000 tons of rubbish a day from the city's 23 central districts. A third of this is burned in nearby dumps. The rest is rushed at the rate of 5000 trips each day through narrow residential streets to the docks, and then transported to a stinking, rat-infested island in Tokyo harbor. (The island's name is *Shin-Yumi-no-Shima*—which, roughly translated, means "The Island of New Dreams.") The city fathers recently decided to reduce the number of daily trips from 5000 to 1000 by using very much larger garbage trucks. But though this may be a bit easier on the ears and nostrils of the Tokyo residents, it will raise as many problems as it solves. Roads will need to be widened at the cost of a reduction in housing, and the widening process will create further waste to dispose of and will involve the city in still more use of energy and building materials. Meanwhile, the city has also designated certain days as "No Car," "No Smoking," and "No Garbage" days. Such measures show to what an extent the inhabitants of Tokyo are concerned about their predicament, but the big problems still remain unsolved.

The United Nations is concerned, too. It has set up an environment program with headquarters in Nairobi, whose purpose is to help guide members in their own urban-planning projects. In 1976, the United Nations Environment Program (to give it its formal name) was scheduled to hold one of the largest international conferences ever. As a result of its studies and preparations for the conference, the U.N. hopes to be able to suggest ways of lessening the pollution and energy-wastage problems that arise from building and inhabiting giant cities, so that the developing nations can avoid the old mistakes when they plan their own futures.

For all of the already industrialized nations, there is a danger, as I have said, in trying to change too much too suddenly. It is easy to condemn creature comforts in general, but not easy to decide which creature comforts are frivolous and harmful, and which are actually basic for modern living. It is extremely difficult to define a standard of living that we can all regard as a minimum consistent with sustaining the natural environment and leaving a world fit for our children and grandchildren. The best that we can do, I think, in considering an individual's responsibility for minimizing the amount of pollution that he and his household inflict upon the world is to judge each case on its own. We can do this if we have a reasonably broad base of agreement on what makes sense and what does not. A couple of examples will show what I mean.

Our massive consumption of food in all the

A pollution of the senses can overwhelm human beings who live and work in big cities. Above: the press of homegoing commuters on London's Oxford Street, where more than 130,000 people come and go every working day. Below: a street in Tokyo, one of the busiest, noisiest, most overcrowded cities in the world.

Left: Central Park—a green oasis in the midst of midtown Manhattan's concrete, steel, and glass desert—is the "lungs" without which many New Yorkers might well be unable to breathe. Physical illnesses, nervous disorders, suicide, and, of course, crime all seem to have roots in the loss of identity suffered by people in urban surroundings.

119

developed countries involves not only the waste that swells our garbage dumps, but also the kind that pollutes our own bodies. We overeat senselessly, and the resultant obesity is one of our most pressing health problems. To cut down on our food, and especially on the rich processed foods in which we increasingly indulge, would not be to do without a basic comfort; it would improve the social environment rather than hurt it. Similarly, we could cut down the crippling incidence of heart disease in our society by changing our attitudes toward such "conveniences" as cigarettes and automobiles. Smoking and lack of exercise certainly work against the good of the heart, but millions of us continue to light up and to take the car on short

errands instead of walking. The fact that many a motorist who prefers to drive, not walk, a few hundred yards will cheerfully spend hundreds of dollars for rowing machines and other kinds of indoor-exercise gadgets is proof that he *knows* he ought to use his muscles and joints more than he does.

As anyone who has ever been forced to spend an hour in a smoke-filled room has certainly discovered, cigarette smoke pollutes the air around the smoker as well as the smoker's own body. And empty cigarette packages lurk among the wild flowers alongside every country lane. Packages, whether of cigarettes or other products, have indeed become the most conspicuous evidence of the way in which our undramatic daily lives adversely affect the environment. A multibillion-dollar industry has become dependent on our habitual waste of material—much of it nondegradable—that contains, wraps, protects, and, above all, dresses up the commodities we buy. In a growing number of instances, especially for pharmaceutical and cosmetic items, we pay more for the package than for the contents. Gradually, all the materials and foodstuffs that used to be sold in loose quantities have been corseted and clothed. Everything from cement to sugar, nuts and bolts to butter, now comes prepacked; invariably we strip off the layers of packaging and throw them all away.

To a limited extent, we *could* make use of the packaging materials. Radio receivers have been constructed in discarded beer cans, children's playthings and art materials reconstituted from used cardboard and paper, indoor plants grown in empty nonreturnable bottles, polystyrene packing used as insulation. But these are merely exceptional possibilities. There are hundreds of materials for which there could be no conceivable use in a modern urban home, and some do more harm to the environment than merely add clutter. For example, acetate film, which is the transparent wrapping most commonly used for outer packaging, produces noxious hydrochloric acid gas when burned. And thousands of tons of it are incinerated every year.

Can we not reclaim garbage for further use if solid wastes are carefully sorted out, as some local authorities in the West have been trying to persuade householders to do? The answer, sadly, is that no successful waste-recycling schemes have yet emerged from pilot attempts. In the first place, most local governments are hard

In Los Angeles, air-pollution figures have reached near-emergency levels, and residents who do not really need to live there have been advised to leave the smog-ridden city.

The modern buildings of Hong Kong typify the way in which Western life styles are supplanting those of once-simpler societies. Too often, however, newly "modernized" cities lack essential facilities. Shortages of water are common; poverty, homelessness, and disease hide behind the new architecture; and untreated sewage pours into harbors such as this one, causing danger and discomfort.

The bizarrely named "Island of New Dreams" off Tokyo, where each day 15,000 tons of garbage are dumped and left to fester. Tokyo's problems of waste disposal are not unique, they are just more conspicuous than in some other major cities. All share the headache of not knowing where to put solid wastes. So far, only conservationists have suggested the obvious answer: produce less rubbish.

As much as half of all food bought in the United States is thrown away. A great deal is probably bought on impulse in the tempting surroundings of supermarkets like this one, and a whole science is devoted to finding ways of persuading customers to buy even more, although it is obvious that they are already overeating. Some of the wasteful buying results from the fact that many necessary items of food can no longer be bought in sufficiently small quantities, because they have been expensively prepackaged in bulk.

No shopper at this early-morning market in Indonesia would buy food he did not need. Earnings are sufficient only to cover essential purchases, and each customer must try hard to spend wisely. There is still competition among traders, of course, but none of the pressures to squander money and materials that cause such extravagant wastefulness in the richer and less sensible West.

pressed to find money and equipment for making rubbish collections of *any* kind; it would be unthinkable to complicate them further by dividing wastes. In the second place, collection and reuse of most wastes (apart from precious metals) has not proved to be financially profitable.

Of course, we could try to persuade manufacturers to package their goods less elaborately, but they could argue with apparent justification, that a return to simpler methods would bring about unemployment. If this argument were carried to its logical conclusion, however, there would never be *any* social changes. We should continue to manufacture cars even after everybody in the world had one; and we could never possibly contemplate disarmament. In the end, such arguments, no matter how apparently justifiable, prove to be false. Similarly, but probably even less justifiably, the manufacturers might also contend that the packaging of food at least protects the public from disease and infection. There is no evidence to support this contention! Instead, there is a likely chance that enthusiastic attempts to "sanitize" natural

objects put us more at risk when the barriers are occasionally dropped. No one wants to see fresh food and meat kept and sold in unhygienic conditions. But there is nothing basically wrong or harmful about good old-fashioned dirt—the sort that drops off a potato when it is picked. It is an irony that a recent case of serious fruit poisoning in Great Britain involved a cargo of apples contaminated with a pesticidal spray and then shrink-wrapped in protective plastic!

Few modern families can grow their own apples, produce their own milk, fell their own timber, reprocess their sewage, or do any of the many other things that would help to cut down waste and reduce pollution. What we can do, however, is continually to press for and support the social changes that will help to bring about environmental improvement. And, as individuals, we can resist the temptation to equate the quality of our own domestic lives with the quantity of our showy, nonessential possessions. "Putting things in the wrong place" is, after all, one possible definition of pollution, even if it does not tell the whole story.

What Can We Do About It?

If there is one thing about pollution that we can be sure of, it is this: we have the power and the knowledge to reduce it. Major obstacles to doing anything, however, are the wide differences of opinion—and sometimes dishonesty—that separate dedicated environmentalists from antagonistic business interests. Each side frequently overstates its case or makes vague pronouncements that serve only to confuse the public. Too often, the opposite sides adopt fixed positions from which they will not budge, whatever the strength of their opponents' arguments. They taunt one another with loaded phrases of disparagement. Environmentalists invariably depict industry as big, bad, and irresponsible; industrialists dismiss the environmental lobby as a collection of unrealistic, amateurish dreamers who, if given their way, would have us live in a world of candles and nut cutlets.

In war, it has been said, the first casualty is the truth, and what has been happening in the environmental debate is that information itself has been polluted. Hearsay, rumor, and guesswork have been allowed to take the place of research, the establishment of facts, and logical thinking. For a variety of reasons, neither industry nor its environmental critics will voluntarily exchange information. Industrialists want to protect their trade secrets, of course; they also have a natural resistance to being thwarted. For instance, if a company has planned an extension of a factory or the introduction of a new process, it is not likely to take kindly to what it sees as the intervention and opposition of meddling do-gooders.

Sometimes, though, the world's industrialists are guilty of sheer laziness and irresponsibility. An example of this is the unloading of industrial wastes. For some years now, they have been routinely dumped either into the sea or wherever there was cheap land available—often on former quarry, open-pit, and mine sites. A lack of supervision or consultation between those disposing of the wastes and official guardians of the public health has led to some spectacular accidents. Not very long ago, a German ship on its way to dump chemical slurry in mid-Atlantic had to be abandoned at sea because several crew members had collapsed through being exposed to leaking

If environmentalists continue to think of industry as rapacious and irresponsible, it is because nauseating eyesores like this copper smelter at Noranda in Canada can be seen all over the world. As a picture of dereliction it would be bad enough, but the cyanide wastes from its activities poison the soil and water for several miles around, and will continue to do so for many years to come.

127

fumes from the ship's holds. It turned out that nobody knew precisely what the ship was carrying—and nobody found out until the originators had been traced and the substance identified. A Finnish ship was halfway to the south Atlantic, where it was to unload a cargo of arsenic waste, when a chance leak of information produced a welter of protest. The Finns were forced to bring the waste back to their country, but the mission could well have gone undetected and the waste would have gone into the sea. As recently as early 1975 (with all we had learned by then about the hazards of chemical wastes), a truck driver in southern England was told to dump surplus sulfuric acid on a certain dumping ground where solid chemicals had previously been unloaded. The driver obeyed orders, and was gassed to death when the sulfuric acid, reacting to the other chemicals, produced hydrogen sulfide.

Every day, poisonous substances with no warning marks of identification are transported by road, rail, sea, and air. And so, although the responsible authorities usually know what is being carried, the people likely to be affected in the event of an accident often do not. Such irresponsible failure to release important information about potential pollutants should, in my view, be a criminal offense. No commercial or national security can justify the deliberate withholding of facts from people put at risk from poisonous materials. Whenever and wherever the air, the water, or the earth is being contaminated or threatened with contamination by government or industry, the individual has a fundamental right to know the nature of the threat.

In some respects, however, well-meaning pressure groups of environmentalists can be at fault. It must be admitted that such groups seldom work with industry to resolve differences of opinion. Instead, they often mount stealthy low-budget investigations, which unearth few really significant facts, or they launch surprise campaigns and attacks on industry, believing this to be a way of "fighting with the enemy's weapons." This concept—the idea that there are enemies—has sadly befogged the public airing of pollution problems. But there is another factor that cannot be ignored. With few exceptions, the environmental lobbyists tend to align themselves with the political Left, and they see their demands for cleaner air and water as part of a wider pressure for social reform and the removal of what they regard as industry's exploitation of labor. Con-

versely, too many men in industry are content to stand on the other side of the political fence and to look upon their pollution-conscious adversaries as a bunch of wild-eyed radicals.

Such dogmatic attitudes, which prevent constructive exchange between the two sides, are hardly justified, particularly in the world as it now is. Western society today is much more a mixture of people than it has ever been, and people increasingly lead what might be called "multiple" lives. Thus, a person may work in one environment, live in another, and spend his leisure hours in yet a third. His view of the world will shift according to which sphere he is occupying at a given time, but the fact remains that the experiences and demands of all these spheres are interrelated. In theory, there ought to be a constantly improved understanding among people along with a more concerted approach to solving common problems.

The industrialist who enjoys fishing, hunting, or simply watching wildlife and sniffing country air must surely know the effects of chemical effluents on the environment. How can he not want to minimize these effects in his own factory? Similarly, the environmentalist who abhors traffic fumes and calls for restraints on private motoring or a moratorium on road building must nevertheless understand how important the automobile is to our economy. And what about the politician who presses on the one hand for reinforced environmental laws and on the other for increased exports? Can he fail to be aware of the obvious fact that there are conflicts between these two objectives? In each case, it makes no sense at all to permit the central issues to be buried under political and economic viewpoints, where no compromise is possible and only extremes are acceptable. Phrases like "You can't have prosperity without pollution" or "Make the polluters pay!" both miss the point.

The point is that pollution can and must be reduced, but that this can be done only by all of us working together. That is why the environmentalists sometimes do their homework more hastily than they should and publicize only such bits of information as will reinforce their views. Just as often, the defenders of industry decline to release any information at all, on the grounds that it is not in the public interest, or else that the public should not be exposed to detailed information, because laymen lack the scientific background necessary for interpreting the data. But if anyone tried to prevent the release of reports about the weather, the balance of payments, unemployment, or sport on similar grounds, the argument would be recognized as absurd. Highly complex facts about all those subjects are discussed regularly in the news media without injury to the public interest.

A government official does not need to be a qualified airline pilot to make decisions affecting airport policy or safety. What he needs is comprehensive information from independent impartial sources. And that is what the public needs if it is to make up its mind about matters that concern the environment. America's Freedom of Information Act is designed to prevent concealment by any organization of information vital to resolving such public disputes as those over nuclear-power-plant siting, oil transshipment by long-distance pipeline, or dumping of chemical wastes. This is a step in the right direction, even though the law is not easily enforceable because a company determined to withhold information can fight its battle in the courts for many months or years. Still, with the recent development of environmental law as a speciality, in the United States, the Freedom of Information Act can be made to work as long as the environmentalists can find money to pay the cost.

There have been moves in the same direction in Europe and Japan. In Britain, there has been pressure—some of it successful—to make governments pay the costs of lawsuits against them for environmental reasons. The argument is that there would have been no litigation if the government had not decided to build a road, clear a forest, dam a river, or whatever, and so it should pay the price for proving its case. And in Japan, private companies have felt compelled by public opinion to make funds available to pollution opponents who wish to fight their claims in court. So the Japanese have come quite a long way since the days of the Minamata disaster, just as the Americans have made real progress since the time of the long-drawn-out conflict between the pesticides industry and the ecologists. In both Japan and America, there used to be little or no specialist legal representation, and there was extreme hostility based on inadequate factual details in a climate of deliberate secrecy. The picture is at least somewhat brighter now.

There is still too much secrecy, though, and environmentalists and consumer-protection bodies are trying to do something about it. Both groups are calling for full labeling of all products so that the public knows their ingredients and properties, and this campaign has been paying off up to a point. But the rate of change and the variety of new substances make it difficult even for official protection agencies to keep track. International trade compounds the problem. Recently, I bought a can of a fluid recommended for the treatment of woodworm. Unlike the creosote-type preparation that was widely used when I was younger, it was formulated from a highly toxic and complex organic pesticide, and users were warned to wear a face mask. They were warned, that is, if they could read French. On the imported can, nothing but basic instructions were printed in English.

Similarly, a well-known oil company markets a solid fly-repellent of which the inhaled vapors may, according to many authorities, be connected with liver disease. In continental Europe it is virtually banned; in the United States it is sold with clear warnings against its use around children and food; in Britain it can be seen dangling in kitchens, bars, and nurseries everywhere. There is no known difference between Holland, the United States, and Britain in our concern for health and safety. We must be using different data in this situation, as in many others.

A very real problem arises, of course, when the facts cannot be ascertained by *anyone*. As we have seen, it is sometimes not possible to determine whether or not a substance is a pollutant until it has been unloaded on the environment. What should we do and say in these circumstances? Or, again, how should we react when two qualified, independent consultants directly refute each other's evidence? My answer is that I honestly believe that if such debates were conducted properly, on the basis of adequate data, we should eventually always arrive at the truth— or, at the very least, our chances of making wildly wrong decisions would be much reduced. The pages of our newspapers are large enough, the power of our television networks sufficient, for us to scrutinize claims and counterclaims more closely than ever before. If we can elect presidents and governments on their showing in the media— and we seem to want it that way—then we can debate far-reaching environmental questions by the same means.

The media are often accused of bias and of preferring to emphasize spectacular or highly emotional issues while giving short shrift to the dull reality. There is some justification for this

We cannot change our ways overnight; equipment such as this machine for spraying insecticide in a California orchard may damage the environment, but it represents thousands of dollars invested in its manufacture and purchase. No one can be asked to abandon such an investment suddenly. Instead, we must gradually evolve less risky methods of solving our most pressing agricultural problems.

serious charge. Popular journalism is looking for good, crisp headlines and dramatic television pictures, and thus sometimes distorts the truth by publicizing only the striking blacks and whites of a pollution story even when the environmentalists themselves are aware of the larger gray areas. In a study of environmental news coverage, conducted at the University of Michigan, the authors concluded that problems were inadequately reported and—more often—ignored until they became crises. Frequently, they said, little attention was paid to the scientific implications of pollution stories. They listed no fewer than a dozen reasons why they thought newspapers and broadcasting stations did not fulfill their environmental responsibilities as public watchdogs. Four of these had to do with the difficulty of assessing the reliability of news sources—from government, conservationists, industrialists, and businessmen. Four involved pressures—time, money, lack of expert opinion, and the fear of

alienating advertisers. Others were reporters' apathy, insufficient space, management hostility to ecology features, and the widespread belief that pollution is a rather "downbeat" issue.

But it is becoming increasingly easy for thoughtful readers and viewers to get all the available facts. In Europe especially, thorough reports of environmental debates are now a common feature of daily life. No important social and political decisions are taken before being extensively reviewed, assessed, criticized, and debated in the media. Lengthy news stories and in-depth analyses on radio and television— sometimes running to individual programs of two hours or more—are devoted to environmental affairs, among other weighty issues. Even in America, where TV viewers are less likely to be asked to sit through long educational programs, the media in general are now paying far more serious attention to such questions as population growth, conservation, and ecological disruption than they were doing only 10 or 15 years ago.

All this has resulted in a greater openness of local debate throughout the West. In America, towns and states have formed committees and groups to decide for themselves what their environmental future ought to be. What, for instance, is the healthiest possible balance between agriculture and industry in a given locale? How much should the demands of tourism be allowed to reduce the number of wilderness areas? How important are those underdeveloped areas to urban man's survival? In Europe, the level of information now available in response to inquiries about road building, afforestation, power, and industrial development has risen sharply. Such developments certainly help to reduce one kind of pollution: the pollution of information, which can do almost as much harm in its way as can more material kinds of poison or filth. An enormous duplication of effort still exists, though, with uncoordinated and often competing organizations putting out reports, holding conferences, mounting campaigns, and adding sometimes to the confusion. A lot of money, time, and paper undoubtedly goes to waste. But a better general understanding of all the facts may delay government and industry in their compulsive hurry to "get things done"; it may also cool off a few of the more hotheaded environmentalists when fallacies in their arguments are revealed. It may lead to a few hurt feelings. But feelings will mend more quickly than the environment.

Meanwhile, there are looming problems that some people might not even recognize as problems yet, because they have enjoyed comparatively little publicity. For instance, many of the official organizations that have been established to protect the environment from man's mistakes are themselves much too subject to conflicting pressures, or else are so enthralled by one aspect of their job that they have a blurred view of its wider implications. The attitude to pest control is one example. Having conceded that the widespread use of such insecticides as DDT can be harmful, many government agencies look not for alternative methods of control, but for chemical alternatives to DDT. It is so easy just to spray crops that both the farmer and those who guide his hands are reluctant to seek new techniques. Moreover, there are companies and individuals that have vested interests in the existing techniques; as a matter of good economics, those interests cannot be ignored. The man who has spent his hard-earned money on a crop-spraying airplane, for example, can hardly be blamed for not wanting to become a lawbreaker overnight if chemical spraying is outlawed.

But the risks must be borne in mind. The search for effective pesticides has veered dangerously toward use of some chemicals that could produce dreaded "super pests" by eliminating weaker strains and producing resistant species. This has already happened with moths, certain weeds, and, to a limited extent, rats. There is only one *right* way to reduce the ecological disruption caused by most chemical pesticides, and that is to gradually eliminate all of them. This is a sad outlook for the agricultural chemical industry; it is bewildering for the farmer; and it means more work for the biologists and botanists. But in the long run there is no other sensible way to cope with this kind of pollution. When pests or plants get out of hand, the reason may be that man has mismanaged the environment. Changes should be made in management methods, not in chemicals.

Antibiotics present a potential problem not unlike that of pesticides. Farmers still use antibiotics to cure certain epidemic diseases (which are only too often diseases that occur especially among animals kept in close proximity, as in intensive rearing units). Increased use leads, of course, to resistance among the organisms that carry the disease, and so the cure becomes less effective. If heavier doses are then administered, there can be a dual result. First, the resistance to disease of the animals themselves is lowered, for the antibiotics may actually destroy beneficial organisms while leaving untouched harmful ones such as salmonellae. Secondly, any human beings that contract diseases passed along the food chain of which the treated animals are a part may fail to respond to antibiotic treatment—and for precisely the same reasons; the typical salmonella organism becomes immune.

Antibiotics are also added to animal feeds as a fattening agent. The mechanisms are not fully understood, but they probably work by killing stomach parasites that would otherwise consume a proportion of the animal's food intake. But the trouble is that we cannot be sure that the antibiotics will select accurately only the truly parasitic organisms. Indeed, we are not yet sure that any stomach organisms in a healthy animal can be called parasites. Some, certainly, are intricately involved in normal digestive processes.

Not enough research has been done to establish

the precise connection, if any, between the above two uses of antibiotics and the incidence of farm-related disease. But sufficient information is at hand to have caused a number of prominent scientists, agriculturists, and medical experts to advise caution. It would be wise to heed their warnings. In recent years, a growing number of hospitals have reported cases where infection has been "transferred" from one species to another; rather, the resistance to treatment has been transferred, which is more alarming. Resistance of typhoid to chloramphenicol, a "sheet-anchor" drug for treating this disease, has spread and grown in incidence over the past decade. In Israel, India, Vietnam, and Mexico, the drug's effectiveness has fallen, and the authoritative British Medical Journal suggests that resistance has been transferred from enteric bacteria arising lower down the animal chain. So a disease that was once curable if detected and treated soon enough could again become one in which one tenth of all the sufferers die.

The same risks, not unnaturally, crop up in the use of antibiotics for treating man himself. Infection can be promoted by intensive use of antibiotics because the ecological effects are exactly parallel to those that permit and encourage the "explosion" of resistant pest species in agriculture. More and more scares in Western hospitals confirm this fact. And the fear of an epidemic that might get out of control is a very real one. Use of colistin, a commonly used broad-spectrum antibiotic, failed to contain an epidemic outbreak of *Klebsiella aerogenes* infection in the neurosurgery unit of a Glasgow (Scotland) hospital. Cases of meningitis became more frequent and less susceptible to treatment by the drug. Extensive modernization and hygiene-monitoring did nothing to improve the situation. But when use of the antibiotic was discontinued, the epidemic came to an end.

Public health conditions in many parts of the world now have a high potential for epidemic disease. Mass international traffic in passengers and freight has raised the risks. So has war, which is usually fought under biologically dangerous conditions, and often by persons who will return to environments with a low resistance to exotic viruses. Modification of the climate through man's activities may also promote disease, especially where such activities result in a drying out of the air, for viruses survive and remain infective in dry air longer than usual.

Antibiotics, finally, present a secondary risk when excreted by human beings who have been treated by them. After passing into groundwater systems, they are absorbed by aquatic organisms, and this makes it possible for disruption to occur further down the life-chain. I know of one self-sufficient farmstead where, because the family's self-sufficiency did not extend to using natural herbal cures during an outbreak of influenza, the antibiotics passed into the waste-disposal system and killed off the beneficial algae that until then had been efficiently processing the family's sewage and helping to produce natural fertilizer for the farm and gas for cooking.

This is the kind of unforeseen reversal to which we might find ourselves exposed through a secondary or even third-hand effect on the natural environment. I have mentioned the risk of nitrate concentrations appearing in water long after the original runoff from fertilizers. Recently, a further hazard has been recognized: highly toxic soil organisms can be brought into contact with man for the first time after being virtually dredged up and concentrated by nitrate action.

Although only a handful of the human race can afford to travel in high-speed style, the environmental convenience may penalize all mankind. Many independent scientists are now convinced that the vapor trails from high-altitude jetliners are stripping away the layers of ozone gas that shield us from harmful ultraviolet rays.

The cause of one case of meningitis in the United States has been identified as a soil-dwelling amoeba introduced in just this manner and transmitted by the humble potato.

And so we see that with antibiotics, as with DDT and similar compounds, substances derived to improve man's chances of survival can backfire and produce countereffects. So can physical changes to the environment. Consider what has happened as a consequence of building the massive Aswan Dam in Egypt, which was designed to produce badly needed electric power and improve irrigation. The unfortunate side effects have included a widespread disruption of local fisheries (and thus a shortage of an important food and export product) and, more worrying, an encouragement of the conditions that promote the parasitic disease bilharziasis. Previously, the disease was kept in check by the fact that the organisms responsible could not flourish during the dry season. Now, in the wide areas surrounding the dam, there is no dry season, and the snails that act as hosts to the bug have proliferated.

A measure of our recent earthly irresponsibility

Disease, defoliation, death, and degradation—all were by-products of the largest high-technology war operation ever mounted: the battle for Vietnam. Bombs, chemicals, and the other modern machines of war are the most brutal of all pollutants.

133

lies in the amount of waste material floating around in outer space. The most advanced applied science that modern man has developed is mirrored in a sky littered with discarded hardware—jettisoned rocket components, burned-out motors, damaged docking equipment, disused satellites, surplus fuel, body wastes, and all the other detritus from the world's space engineering. The muck extends throughout the solar system and beyond. Some of it is unavoidable, naturally, in view of humanity's determination to ride out into space: but to judge from a reading of the technical literature on freely orbiting junk, the main risk as the technologists see it, is that some of it might collide with future spacecraft. There appears to be no strong feeling that to make a technological dump of outer space just might be unethical. For the time being, the issue is not a dramatic one, because space exploration has slowed down, but it does raise doubts about our collective good intentions. It also reinforces a widespread belief that high technology is frequently the worst of environmental culprits.

With most technological improvements, in

fact, there are undesirable environmental side effects. Fungicides applied to crops bring the risk of mercury methyl poisoning; aircraft carry disease from one side of the earth to the other. The fastest airplanes—the supersonic variety—fly so high that they may well disrupt the natural ozone content of the upper atmosphere by the action of their nitrogen-oxide-containing vapor trails; and many scientists are strongly of the opinion that climatic changes are taking place as a result. Similar alarm has even been expressed about the effects of the comparatively humble

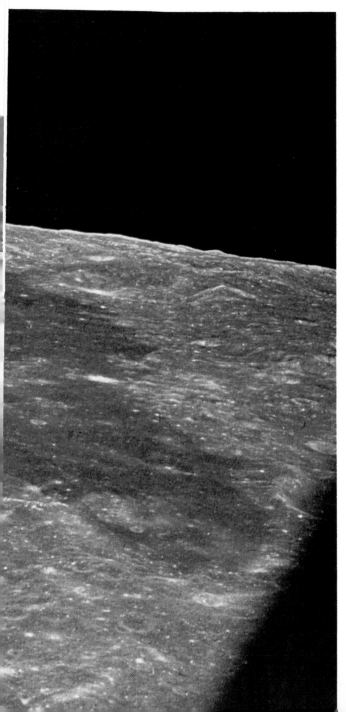

aerosol spray, hundreds of millions of which are now in common use. The most widely used propellant in aerosol cans is a gas called chlorofluoromethane. Scientists at the National Academy of Sciences in the United States are so concerned about the threat of this gas to the natural ozone in the upper atmosphere—and the consequent possible rupture of our global safeguard against high-level ultraviolet radiation—that they have begun an urgent experimental program to study the mechanisms involved.

But what can they do if their investigation suggests that a crisis point is being approached? Should they call a ban on aerosols or press for the use of a different gas? In fact, the chlorofluoromethane itself has replaced another, more locally hazardous propellant that was used in early aerosols. What other, less risky gas might now be available? As for banning aerosol sprays—well, once again we are up against the question of ecology in conflict with the social and industrial habits of the modern world. And in times of industrial difficulty there is an understandable tendency to reverse many of the environmental advances achieved in prosperous years. Thus, for instance, the date by which American and European car manufacturers were required to improve emission controls was pushed further and further away during the mid-1970s, when it became hard to sell *any* cars, let alone ones that were fitted with several hundred dollars' worth of antipollution equipment.

The economic argument also won out over the ecological as it concerned schedules for removing lead from gasoline, installing extra smoke-scrubbing elements in factory chimneys, withholding effluent from rivers, and recycling garbage. When times are hard in industrialized countries, the stimulus is always to produce more, not less, at almost any cost to the environment. So it seems self-evident that what we really need is a *new* economics, one that would take account, whether in times of prosperity or economic depression, of the environmental costs, and would measure them in sharp, comprehensible terms.

I can think of several ways to introduce such a system. One might be to build an environmental tax into the total cost of every commodity and

By reaching out to the solar system and beyond, 20th-century man has created an entirely new environment, and littered it. This lunar module is only one of scores of vehicles and components that now float endlessly in outer space.

Picture Credits

Key to position of picture on page: (B) bottom, (C) center, (L) left, (R) right, (T) top; hence (BR) bottom right, (CL) center left etc.

144

EARTH IN DANGER

Part 2
Conservation

by Michael Crawford

Père David's deer—a Chinese species saved from extinction by the establishment of this herd at Woburn Park in England.

Series Coordinator   Geoffrey Rogers
Series Art Director   Frank Fry
Design Consultant   Guenther Radtke
Editorial Consultant   Donald Berwick
Series Consultant   Malcolm Ross-Macdonald
Art Editor   Susan Cook
Editors   Damian Grint
Maureen Cartwright
Research   Barbara Fraser

Contents: Part 2

Editorial Advisers

DAVID ATTENBOROUGH Naturalist and Broadcaster
MICHAEL BOORER, B.SC. Author, Lecturer, and Broadcaster

Conservation in Perspective

It should be understood that we in our time are no worse as plunderers of nature than were our ancestors; it is just that there are more of us and we have more efficient ways to plunder. To understand conservation and the need for it, we must begin by looking at history, which tells us that man has always been an exploiter: not just of natural resources but of his own kind.

Five thousand years ago, the island of Crete was settled by a people who seem to have had connections with Anatolia (a region of modern Turkey), whence they brought livestock, crop seeds, and plants. Already excellent navigators and sailors, these Minoans were attracted to Crete by its forests of cypress, cedar, and deciduous trees, and they eventually became a powerful trading nation, the very hub of activity in the Mediterranean. The remains of the palace at Knossos provide us with a glimpse of their remarkably advanced civilization, with its vividly conceived architecture and art as well as its creature comforts such as flush toilets (which our own civilization has generally enjoyed only since the mid-19th century). But the success of their merchant navy, which placed them in economic command of the Mediterranean, depended on ships; the ships depended on wood; and the wood came from the deciduous forests that lined the island's shores and clothed its hills. Eventually, there were few trees still growing in Crete.

Forest exploitation and clearance made way for agriculture, upon which the expanding population increasingly depended. Thick woodlands on the hillsides were replaced by olives. But the olive tree has a shallow root network, and its thin gray leaves contribute little water to the hot environment. Replacement of the deeprooted, broadleaved trees led to a lack of moisture in the air and of nutrients in the topsoil, and discouraged the growth of small plants, and so the topsoil in olive groves was exposed to erosion.

Bald hills flank Athens as natural monuments to man's misuse of the land. Forest clearance and overgrazing in the days of ancient Greece triggered off erosion from which the hillside soil has never recovered sufficiently to support trees. Nowadays, mankind is plundering soils and wildlife all over the world.

12

That was what happened in ancient Crete. Rain washed topsoil from the slopes into the sea, and bared rocks attracted and stored the sun's heat and dried out the remaining earth. Ultimately, even agriculture failed, and a weakened nation fell prey to pirates and robbers. Time drew a curtain over the history of the Minoans until, in the early 1900s, Sir Arthur Evans found the palace of Knossos buried in topsoil and dust.

Nearly 1000 years after the end of Minoan Crete, Plato warned his fellow-Greeks of the devastation to animal life and agriculture that would follow if the reckless practice of cutting down the forests on the hills around Athens continued. But deforestation continued. With little evaporative water loss from broad leaves to maintain local humidity, and with almost no litter or humus from fallen leaves to replenish it, the topsoil was washed and blown away. Now there are no forests and no trees around Athens,

and no topsoil for them to take root in, anyway—only barren, eroded hillsides of exposed rocks and small pockets of barely arable earth on which some form of residual agriculture is still practiced. Neither the Minoan nor the classical Greek forests could be replenished today.

Thousands or even hundreds of years ago, when man could no longer wrest a living from his homeland he could always find somewhere else to go. The Romans spread across Europe, and after the collapse of the Roman Empire, expansion continued in northern Europe and across the water to Britain. The Vikings in their ships went to Iceland and Greenland. The Crusaders marched eastward; and Columbus sailed westward and discovered a whole new world. The riches of America lay open to endless exploitation, with nothing standing in the way of the European except a relatively small number of "ignorant" native peoples. And so, coming face

Once, forests fringed much of the Mediterranean Sea. But these two typically Mediterranean scenes show ways in which man has remodeled the environment. Left: dry-stone walls shore up a steep hillside in Cyprus. Without them, soil deprived of its ancient forest cover would swiftly wash away in the winter rains. Right: olive groves and citrus orchards—often doubling as wheatfields—now take up huge tracts of land once occupied by cork oak and other evergreens. Here, in Andalusia, is much of Spain's most fertile farmland. Yet here, too, careless land use in dry places produces its areas of scrub and semidesert.

Two old pictures recall the confrontation when an Old World civilization began to put its stamp on civilizations of the New World. Above: the famous meeting between the Spanish conqueror of Mexico, Hernando Cortes, dressed in the armor of a European knight, and the Aztec emperor, Montezuma, surrounded by the royal panoply of ancient Mexico. As in Peru, very much farther south, the Europeans made a friendly meeting just an overture to savage exploitation of people less well armed than themselves. Left: Cortes' Spaniards massacring Indians at Cholula as a punishment for an alleged Indian plan to murder their Spanish masters.

ing to Inca legend, Kon-Tiki Viracocha, the Creator God, had temporarily abandoned his people but would one day return; and Atahualpa thought that the Spaniards were representatives of Viracocha who would preside over his investiture. So the young Inca ruler met the Spaniards unarmed in a show of honor and trust—whereupon the civilized Europeans seized him and massacred his 10,000 followers, finding nothing shameful in this treatment, because (after all) the Indians were not Christians. Atahualpa tried in vain to buy his release. So much gold was brought to the interlopers that it filled a whole room, and the Spaniards were delighted. In return for this windfall they burned the trusting Sun King at the stake, but it is said that they generously spared him the fire by strangling him first as a reward for embracing Christianity. Such cruelty of man to man stands as an extreme example of humanity's willingness—indeed, determination—to waste *all* the earth's resources, including entire human cultures.

In North America, the indigenous Indian has been almost exterminated. In Tasmania, the natives used to be shot dead as a kind of sport; I was somehow reminded of this when, in 1973, I read newspaper reports of an Australian football team that enjoyed a "day's outing" shooting at kangaroos, just for the fun of it. Although many Aborigines remain in Australia, they too were once hounded almost as badly as the Tasmanian natives. In South America, forest clearance is still allegedly accompanied here and there by wholesale shooting of native tribes that get in the way. These are examples of our rejection of the conservation principle even as it applies to human blood. Yet they are part of history, and a clear view of history is essential to an understanding of the forces that make man do what he does.

The slave trade provides another example in the history of exploitation; "civilized" people stole men, women, and children from their native lands of Africa and sold them to the West Indies, North America, Europe, and Arabia. In all, over 2 million human beings survived the crossing of the Atlantic and became slaves in the New World. Probably between two and three times that number died during attacks on their villages, or on the cruel journey over land and across the ocean.

In the eastern part of Africa, pitiful caravans of human merchandise converged on the trail

to face with a human brother from whom he had been separated by geological processes for many thousands of years, the European explorer knew precisely what to do: exploit the people as well as their land.

Perhaps the most ruthless instance of such exploitation was the total destruction of the Inca civilization by the Spaniards in the middle years of the 16th century. When a band of Spaniards led by Francisco Pizarro landed on the west coast of South America in 1532, news spread rapidly to young Atahualpa, who was passing through Cajamarca, in what is now Peru, on his way to be installed as Inca, or Sun King. Accord-

from Dodoma in the heart of Tanzania to Baga-moyo on the coast. Hundreds of individuals were locked together in small, airless prisons before being sold in the marketplace and transported in chains for use by the sultans of Arabia. If you have ever wondered, by the way, why there is such a large African population in the United States and the West Indies and not in Arabia, the answer is simple: in America it was hoped that unrestricted breeding of the slaves would increase the labor force, and it did; the Arabians, on the other hand, simply castrated all males, young or adult.

In our own century, mass killings of Jews, Biafrans, and other peoples bear further testimony to man's inhumanity to man. So it is hardly surprising that the callousness of the human race toward its own species should have been paralleled throughout history by an even more savage disregard for nature. The destruction of wildlife in Europe spanned a number of centuries. In Scotland, for instance, the brown bear became

No one knows how many Indians lived in North America before the arrival of Europeans. It was certainly many millions. But as the whites advanced westward across the continent, the Indians were systematically destroyed. Many were massacred in battle. Some were exterminated through being infected with smallpox. The few survivors were driven from their ancestral lands and forced to settle on reservations where the ground was so poor that no white settler wanted to make use of it. Even those reserves were not safe for them. Of the 138 million acres allocated to Indian peoples in 1887, over half was taken from them during the following 50 years. Most tribes simply died out altogether. The Navahos, however, were the exception. In 1863, virtually the entire tribe was compelled by the Army to march 300 miles into imprisonment at Fort Sumner. When they were released four years later, they were sent to a reservation in the desert of Arizona and New Mexico. Yet in spite of these cruel hardships and humiliations, they survived. Today, there are more Navahos than there were in the 18th century. They number some 100,000 and are the most numerous of all surviving Indian groups in North America. They have adapted themselves with great success to the ways of the white man. Here they are seen at one of their local election meetings. They discovered that their reservation lands, agriculturally so poor, were rich in minerals and oil, and they negotiated the sale of the rights very profitably. Their tribal council has even installed a computer to assist it in handling their business affairs. They are a spectacular example of how a tribal people can retain their identity and much of their tribal culture and yet also come to terms with the modern world.

18

extinct in the 9th or 10th century, reindeer sometime between the 12th and 14th centuries, wild boar in the 14th or 15th century, and the wolf in the 18th century. By the beginning of our own century there was little left except rabbits and deer. Most of the indigenous forests had gone from Scotland by 1900, too; for example, all the oaks in two counties had been stripped in the 17th century just to build one large warship. This sort of thing happened all over Britain, in fact. Today many areas on the map are marked as the forest of so-and-so, but when you arrive at the forest of so-and-so, all you see is a bracken desert. And, of course, when the forests went, wild animals and plants went with them.

Similarly, North America was alive with wild animals, and the east coast thick with forests, only 150 years ago. The excitement of such wealth was too much; the hunter and predator instincts in the new American settlers—instincts that had gradually become suppressed by life in overexploited Europe—burst to the surface. This

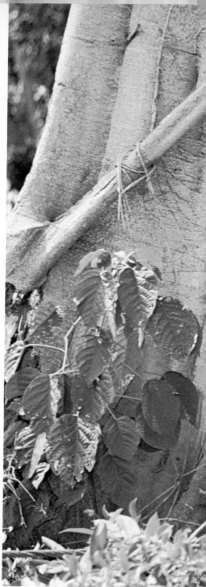

The pictures on these pages show trees being "harvested" in different parts of the world for man's needs. Left: stacking radiater pines in Whaka State Forest, New Zealand. Above: timber cutting in Indonesia. Right: Canadian lumberjacks floating logs in Quebec. Forestry conservation is a high priority on the list of man's needs. Although in such countries as Canada, forestry conservation principles are acted upon, in the majority of countries those responsible for forest conservation think largely in terms of a monoculture of softwoods. The idea of managing diverse forests and farming them for timber, fuel, seed oils, and honey does not seem to have been considered. Yet there is no reason why mixed forests of hardwood and softwood trees should not be commercially viable. Too many reforestation programs betray the short-sighted thinking of the exploiter looking for quick returns, and no higher principles are considered.

great philosophical and religious systems. At the roots of our search for truth lies an urge to do the "right" thing: to distinguish between good and evil. In fact, conservation is intimately involved with moral questions. What right has one man to destroy a natural resource; what right has one man or one group of people to destroy scenery that would otherwise provide enjoyment and inspiration for thousands of others. What right have people, local authorities, and industries to discard their raw excrement into the atmosphere, the soil, the rivers, lakes, and estuaries, and the oceans, so destroying the wildlife upon which many depend. What right

has man to exterminate a species of plant or animal life whose unique genetic makeup provides interest or may even be of use and survival value to future generations?

Clearly no man has the right to exterminate life or beauty from which others obtain enjoyment or benefit, and clearly no man has the right to poison the earth and oceans on which we and our children depend. Consequently such actions must be immoral.

Western moral philosophy of the past had its roots in the Judaeo-Christian ethic, which defined the moral code in precise terms backed by the authority of God. The moral code of what was

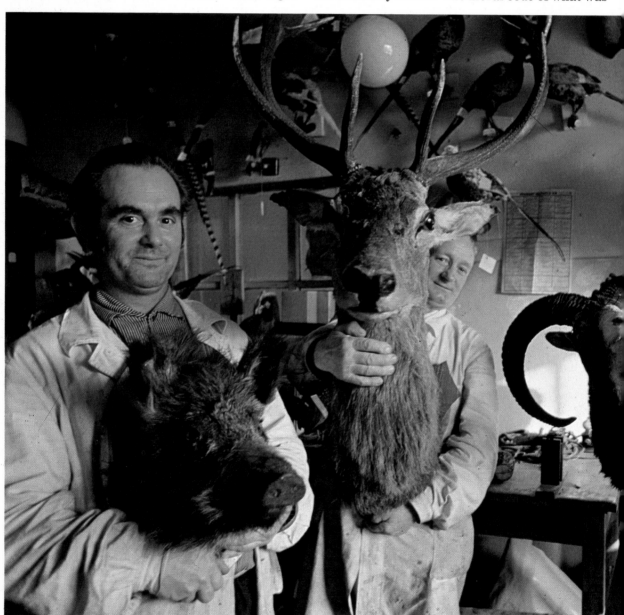

right or wrong was derived from God's own commandments.

At the same time others attempted to construct a framework for moral philosophy that did not lean on the authority of a God, but that was based on *a priori* reasoning. The German philosopher Kant, for example, argued that if you did not bring the authority of God into the discussion there had to be some fundamental reason or principle by which an action could be judged as "right" or "wrong:" he refers to this as a "categorical imperative." An important test of moral judgment used by Kant was to universalize an action and examine whether it was then consistent with humanity: for example, wholesale crime can easily be understood as wrong because if universalized it will destroy humanity and society. Although this is a gross oversimplification of Kant's moral philosophy the connection with conservation can easily be recognized. Actions that lead to the destruction of wildlife are morally wrong because they adversely affect the many who depend on it. At one extreme such actions threaten the livelihood of fishermen and those who depend on them for food. At another extreme, these actions remove for all time the pleasure and intellectual stimulation to be obtained from that which is beautiful.

Man the world over has plundered nature's wildlife treasury merely for trophies and to satisfy the vagaries of fashion. Left: splendid samples of Czechoslovakia's big wild mammals displayed as hunters like to see them—heads shorn of their bodies. Above: reptile skins, remodeled as handbags and shoes, adorn a Singapore store.

Although we can recognize the implications of moral philosophy to conservation, the Judaeo-Christian ethic in particular drew a dividing line between man and other animals: man possessed a soul and was built in God's likeness. Indeed both the Christian and the Western humanist philosophies discussed the moral law in terms of the actions of one man to another. I would suggest that the conservation ethic is an extension of those philosophies to embrace the action of man to nature. In fact, in my view the conservation philosophy goes further than previous Western philosophies because it is concerned with actions and attitudes of human beings toward man, nature, the world, and the future.

Such an approach to conservation demon-strates the distinction between conservation and preservation. We preserve a building, a painting, or a dead tissue in a museum; we conserve living systems and the habitats on which they depend. The difference becomes clear if we think of the common practice of preserving tapeworms in formalin for medical museums. We do not "conserve" tapeworms. Preservation is a simple action; whereas conservation implies an attitude that involves active *management* of the thing conserved. A museum specimen—George Washington's house or a painting in the Louvre—is preserved as nearly as possible in its original form, but this cannot be done with creatures that belong to the biological world, for biology is concerned with change. Living things are born,

grow up, reproduce, and die; populations of species grow if conditions are favorable, and their growth affects other species, so that the balance of the living world keeps changing. Hence, if we are to conserve living things with a certain amount of discrimination, we must interfere with the biological world through a system of careful management.

In its full sense, the extension of the realm of moral and economic philosophy to biology gives us our highest reason for conservation: it is morally wrong *for us* to destroy species. However, nature herself does exterminate species. Thus, in practicing conservation, we must obviously interfere with the natural process of evolution. This is, indeed, a rather disturbing paradox, but

the essence of the paradox can be appreciated if we consider a few of the well-known facts about evolutionary history.

Several thousand million years ago, the Precambrian oceans predominantly supported blue-green algae, which, like all green plants, excrete oxygen as an end product of their metabolic processes. These living systems dominated the world for over 2500 million years, but slowly they succumbed to the force of evolution and biological change. As the blue-green algae polluted their own atmosphere with oxygen, the amount of oxygen in the oceans and the atmosphere rose, and the environment became less suitable for them. Meanwhile, by making more and more oxygen available, they were encouraging the

evolution of oxygen-breathing life forms. And so the blue-green algae relinquished their domination of the world's oceans to a great diversity of competing organisms.

The collapse of the blue-green algae could have been avoided, had a galactic conservation lobby decided to manage their survival. All it needed was a system to withdraw the oxygen from the environment as it was produced, in order to prevent the blue-green algae's virtual self-destruction by atmospheric pollution with oxygen. Needless to say, we owe our presence here today to the fact that there was no such galactic conservation society—or that, if there was, it preferred not to interfere with the natural processes of biology.

The era of dominant trilobites (small, fierce-looking, crustaceanlike creatures) followed the collapse of the blue-green algae. We do not know why they vanished, but we do know that the next dominant species in the early oceans, the graptolites, were quite different in looks and character. The graptolites were delicate, beautiful, and eminently worth conserving, but disappeared

Far left: although this village pond with its burden of trash is in Spain, it is a sight all too common in a number of industrialized countries. Rarer nowadays are the unsightly garbage dumps in city centers, as pictured below in wealthy Lagos, capital of Nigeria, although it is in large urban areas that such vast quantities of waste originate. Much can be done to clean up these eyesores though, and spontaneous groups of people have donated their time and enthusiasm to rehabilitating village ponds. On a larger scale, local government organization can be persuaded to recover scarred countryside as has happened with this landscaped gravel pit in England (left).

after reaching a zenith that enables us still to find evidence of their numbers in fossilized tracings from one end of the earth to the other. When, eventually, the land was colonized, great gingkos and enormous insects and giant reptiles enjoyed an ecosystem unparalleled in its grandeur. That grandeur, characterized by enormous leafy trees and shrubs and huge dinosaurs, reached a peak and disintegrated; it was replaced by smaller flowering and seed-bearing plants, and then followed by the evolution of mammals.

Evolution, then, is a continuous history of rise and fall. From the beginning, the collapse of one reign and the extinction or near-extinction of the dominant life form have always given way to the emergence of another system. Dominance has inevitably led to extinction. Hence the conservationist paradox: because the conservation principle obstructs change, it is antibiology, for change is the essence of biology; yet the conservationist is passionately committed to biological nature! The only way to resolve the resultant dilemma is to accept the view that our activities for conservation contribute to the battle for maintaining ourselves as the dominant species. Either man or nature is in control; left to herself, nature will topple us from our pedestal. We *must*, therefore, control the situation by management, or perish.

Conservation is often thought of as a move to save endangered species, but let us examine the question of endangered species from a realistic point of view. In the immediate past, the mammals have had a history of great diversity in the size of individuals and the number of individuals within the various species. The primates emerged late, and hominoid apes later, with man emerging about 2 to 4 million years ago. Then came the extinction of vast numbers of large mammals during what is called the "Pleistocene Overkill," perhaps 8000 to 12,000 years ago.

Thereafter, animal and plant domestication emerged, probably in response to the increasing human population and the already growing

Below: camels at Karachi, Pakistan. Right: halfbreed dingo dog in the door of a banana packing shed in New South Wales, Australia. In most of the world, domesticated animals that man uses for such purposes as draft, food, guarding, and clothing now live where big, wild mammals once roamed before Stone Age hunters killed them off in the search for food.

The Interdependence of Living Things

Constructing the Trans-Amazonian Highway, then clearing road-side forest, and establishing farm plants and animals seems simple. Yet no one really knows the dangers or for how long it will work. We do not yet really know to what extent we rely on the photosynthesis of these great forests.

That nature balances her own books is a popular misconception; because biology is concerned with change, there can never be a permanent balance in nature. Nonetheless, long periods of apparent stability do occur, when some kind of balance seems to operate. It is that limited degree of balance that we have to understand if—unlike the dinosaurs or the trilobites—our species is to survive. And in order to be able to understand this balance, we must be thoroughly aware of

the way in which living systems are interlocked.

In any diverse wildlife population, the collaboration of different species works to a truly remarkable extent, and this collaboration is intimately woven around such basic biological needs as food, water, and survival through reproduction. Only too often we have learned lessons about this interdependence as a result of man breaking a link in the chain either through the selective killing of one species or through the development of agricultural systems that destroy natural habitats. Some ambitious men learned just such a lesson—a lesson about the interdependence of plants and insects—a few years ago during a large-scale attempt to farm sunflowers in Tanzania for their seeds and oil.

In preparing an enormous plot of land for planting, bulldozers cleared away all the trees and bushes. During this operation, bees were a constant and frightening nuisance; violently

Peo
con
Her
(ab
leth
adr
an e
pois
and

late arrival was the bagworm, which is very resistant to insecticides and can make short work of trees by stripping leaves so effectively that the tree often dies.

By this time, concentrations of insecticides in the area were so high that any produce would almost certainly have been unfit for human consumption. With the leaves, the fruits, and the trunks of the trees all being attacked simultaneously, the plantation was virtually abandoned in despair. Then, when all seemed lost and backs were turned, a parasite attacked one of the leaf-eating caterpillars, and hordes of wasps came in and gorged themselves on larvae of all sorts. In effect, the wasps reestablished a herbivore/carnivore regulation process, and the problem

Laboratory workers examining a barn owl's liver at the Nature Conservancy's Experimental Station near Huntingdon in England. Chemical analysis revealed significant amounts of residues of the powerful organic chlorine pesticides DDT and dieldrin. Grain treated with these chemicals probably became food for mice that fell prey to the owl. Thus persistent poisons pass along a food chain, their concentration increasing with each animal link. One result is breeding failures among the birds of prey affected.

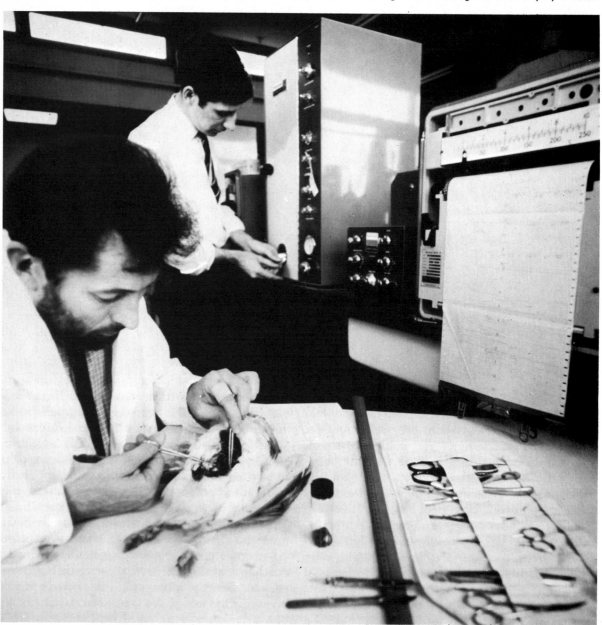

Agricultural improvement sometimes brings unforeseen hazards requiring intensive efforts to remove them. Harnessing the Nile for irrigation has indirectly spread bilharziasis, a disease that weakens millions of people in North Africa and Southwest Asia. Here, Sudanese men are dipping bags of copper sulfate into an irrigation canal near the White Nile. This poison kills the water snails harboring parasites that cause bilharziasis. But the poison is also bound to kill countless innocuous kinds of water organism.

was cut down to manageable size. Today the plantation is a going concern. Seriously affected trees are cut down and burned, and insecticides are used only very selectively. Thus, a combination of biological control, physical control, and a carefully localized and limited use of insecticides has produced a viable answer to what seemed an insoluble problem.

There can be little doubt that pesticides do pose a threat to conservation. Because many are nondegradable, they accumulate in the food chain and are therefore a real menace to such top carnivores as large birds of prey. The conservationists have been accused of overstating the size of the threat. Still, even if they *have* perhaps overreacted, it is also true that their strictures have prevented large chemical companies from cashing in on too many reckless and disastrous policies. As a result of pressure from such people as the late Rachel Carson, we now have highly selective pesticides that will kill aphids, for example, but are harmless to the ladybug that feeds on them.

Insect activity is, of course, not confined to the demolition of man's houses, crops, and health.

Insects play a positive role in food production, maintaining genetic diversity in plants, recycling rubbish, and generally tidying up the forest floor. The evolution of bright colors for flowers probably had its origin in the need to attract insects for pollination. Without such creatures as bees and butterflies, seed production and genetic diversity among the plants would be well-nigh impossible. And so would the survival of the vertebrates, because insects are an important source of food. Frogs, lizards, and salamanders patiently wait for flying insects at the water's edge. Hedgehogs, badgers, foxes, and nearly all small primates enjoy the larger insects. A chimpanzee will poke a twig down into a termite nest until it is covered, and will devour stickful after stickful of the tasty creatures, looking a bit like a child sucking a lollipop, except that the insects are decidedly more nutritious. Small birds catch insects on the wing; there are few more fascinating sights than the sight of swallows attacking a swarm of flying ants. The continuous thread of interdependence from tiny insect to large animal is lengthened as the small birds, frogs, and rodents that eat

Termites (shown enlarged) are antlike tropical insects that feed on wood, leaves, and waste substances as well as wooden posts and houses. But they are a valued food source for Africans.

insects are in their turn preyed upon by owls, hawks, and eagles.

Even man has always eaten insects or their produce. We of the Western world, of course, confine our insect food to honey, but it is a different story elsewhere. Africans build simple wooden frames over termite nests, covering the nest with a cloth as soon as it begins to swarm, so as to trap substantial amounts of a highly nutritious food. Another kind of trap—this time for locusts or grasshoppers—is the modern tropical city itself. In the swarming season, the plump hoppers are attracted at night by bright street lights, against which they break their fragile wings; when they fall to the ground, they are scooped up in handfuls by the street crowds. It is hard to say whether the gaiety of such occasions is stimulated by the free food trapped

by city lights, by the thought of the delicacy in the frying pan (they taste like a cross between deep-fried shrimps and whitebait), or by the money that can be made from selling the surplus in the local market.

Another aspect of insect life relevant to the interaction issue is the role that they play in clearing away debris. Ants devour carcasses of dead animals, cleaning the bones inside and out and thus preventing the incubation and transmission of infectious disease. Beetles and termites help to clear away dead leaves, branches, and even whole trees. One remarkable creature, the dung beetle, spends much of its life clearing up the dung left by large animals. The female of the species rolls the dung into balls many times her own size. Then she and her male partner dig a hole and live underground with the supply of dung, which provides food for beetles and larvae during the time of year when the surface is inhospitable. These creatures are more than just an amusing curiosity, for they

have an important ecological function apart from the general business of keeping the earth tidy. In Australia, where neither cattle nor dung beetles are indigenous, it has recently been realized that there is no effective ecological system for removing the excrement of the cattle and sheep that the white man brought with him to that continent. The authorities have been investigating the possibility of introducing dung beetles into the country. Someone has suggested that the dung beetle could be the savior of Australian agriculture. Although that is an extreme view, there is an element of truth in it, and it illustrates one aspect of the interdependence of living systems, as well as the sometimes unrecognized value to man of even the unlikeliest organisms.

The role of insects is generally overlooked in conservation thinking and planning. This is one reason why I have chosen to discuss them at some length, rather than larger animals whose functions and interactions are more familiar

Dung beetles shape dung into balls that they bury as food for their young. In this way they distribute fertilizer and, in dry soils, help to perform an earthworm's soil-mixing function.

to most readers. Modern approaches to agriculture often overlook insects that are classified as harmful! Agricultural practice first destroys the habitat of ants, beetles, bees, butterflies, and wasps, all of which are heavily dependent on their habitat for breeding grounds. The destruction of insect homes, the poisoning of the insects themselves, and the consequent dwindling of their numbers mean the disruption of a vital food supply for other animals and the failure of nearby undeveloped regions to maintain plant diversity. If there are no insects, there is no cross-pollination of plants and little food for birds, which are essential agents of seed dispersal: they carry the seeds of the vegetation they have eaten and plant them literally here, there, and everywhere in their droppings. The thesis of *The Silent Spring* is that insecticides kill the insects, as a consequence

47

of which bird life is threatened. That may be true, but habitat destruction by modern agricultural practice is a more important negative factor in the long run than insecticides. Indeed, the loss of pollinating and pest-controlling insects through habitat destruction could be far more disastrous than even Rachel Carson envisaged.

Similarly, forestry organizations the world over have not yet fully realized the ecological impact of their monoculture policies. Nor do town planners consider the effect of their flower-garden or tree-planting activities on insect life, even if they are enlightened enough to plant trees and flowers. For a vivid idea of the enormous influence that monoculture agriculture, forestry, and town planting can have on insect life, let us consider the normal life style of the honeybee. The worker bee gathers nectar and pollen from flowers, and these are stored in honeycombs, where the nectar is turned into honey. Young nurse bees feed both honey and pollen to the growing larvae in the combs, and the continuing propagation of the bee colony is dependent on the assured creation of new queens whenever a hive becomes overcrowded or the old queen loses her ability to lay eggs. When that happens, the nurse bees and workers build some extra large cavities in the comb, and the queen lays ordinary worker eggs in them. The larvae are then fed on royal jelly, which is a special form of bee milk, and one simple worker egg turns into a magnificent queen. Either the new queen then kills the old queen, or the old queen leads a swarm of bees from the hive to start a new nest elsewhere. The new queen will certainly sting to death any as yet unhatched sister queens, as only one queen can rule the hive, and the extra queen cells are there in case of failure.

The survival of the species is dependent on the queen and the workers; only the queen lays the eggs, but the workers attend to the rearing of the grubs. For a colony to survive from one year to the next, it must, in the springtime, have a healthy, active queen and plenty of workers to attend to the eggs and brood. For this to happen, enough stores of honey and pollen must have been laid in during the preceding

Even a small city garden can eclipse most country woods and meadows for the size and brightness of its blooms. But because city gardens are planned to appeal to man, the modest flowers that many pollinating insects require are absent from them, and the insects dependent on such flowers are therefore also missing.

49

Bees (below) feed pollen and honey made from nectar to bee larvae in a honeycomb. In gathering food, bees pollinate flowering plants, thus fertilizing seeds. This colony of beehives in Mexico (right) can thrive only because nectar is obtainable throughout the breeding season from different plants that flower in succession.

season to see the bees well through the winter. An active queen bee can lay up to 3000 eggs a day, and a healthy hive may build up to a strength of 50,000 bees. To build up such a colony after the ravages of winter takes time, vigor, and a good store of basic supplies. It usually takes about 21 days from the laying of the egg until the adult worker bee emerges.

Under natural conditions, nectar and pollen are available throughout the spring, summer, and early fall, and some winter flowers also furnish food for bees on warm days in very temperate climates. The season starts with pollen-bearing willows, crocuses, and other early-flowering plants, which lead in to fruit blossoms, then mayflowers and hawthorns. There follows a short but profuse flow of nectar from such trees as the sycamore, succeeded by the privets and linden trees, and finally the clover and heather. To build the powerful worker force requires a continuous supply of food, which means that bees cannot survive unless nectar is available throughout the season. If only one plant species exists in an area, no matter how profuse its provision of pollen and nectar, there is not enough time for the bees to increase their numbers and to gather adequate food supplies for the winter. And so a monoculture cannot support bees; and in different ways and for different reasons it is unable to support any of the other kinds of pollinating insects, either.

Urban planners often line roads with one

species of tree. Forest clearance and reforestation programs replace diversity with a monoculture of pines. Most garden lovers plant brightly developed flowers that have been bred by man's ingenuity for their floral attributes, with so many petals that even if the plant could put some effort into nectar production instead of show, neither butterfly nor honeybee could gain access to it. Some artificial plantings can be seen as ecological disasters, because the threat to useful insects is a threat to all life on the land. But it is not just insects that are the victims of monoculture thinking; the plants themselves also suffer as a result.

A great belt of rain forest lines the slopes of Mount Kilimanjaro in Tanzania. Some years ago, expert opinion decided that this could become a rich source of timber. The fastest-growing timber is pine, but the forest was composed mainly of varieties of mahogany, fig, and olive trees. The experts solved the problem by letting the local people cut down the existing trees in one large area for firewood and house building, after which they were permitted to grow corn there for four years. Thereafter the place was entirely given over to pine trees. But although Africa is a hot place, rain forests can be cool. Much of the root system is very deep and feeds off deep water tables. Broadleaved trees evaporate water and help to cool the air by extracting heat in the form of heat vaporization: the "rain trees" actually drip water. Pines, by contrast, are shallow-rooted and have a low rate of water loss from the needles; they are also resinous and highly inflammable. No sooner had the pine trees become established than the African heat became too much for them. Thousands of acres went up in a fierce blaze that ate into the surrounding rain forest.

All life on land has depended on the world's forests for much of the recycling of oxygen and minerals. We really do not know what the effects of replacing many of these forests by agricultural land or shallow-rooted trees may be. Certainly, much wildlife is directly dependent on forest habitats, but we cannot be sure how dependent *we* are on their photosynthesis and mineral-recycling activities. In my view, this question gets too little attention from conservationists, who usually emphasize the need for protecting rare plant species. Thus we create conservation areas for the sake of alpine plants such as *Primula scotia* or *Silene acaulis*, build a six-foot fence around the one surviving "military orchid" in England, or establish botanical gardens to breed and demonstrate exotic plants. But such actions basically concern species that are colorful, unusual, or pretty to look at: *Camellia granthamiana*, when there was only one such tree left in Hong Kong; the *coral cup*, so rare that it is confined to the Table Mountain of South Africa; the giant buttercup of the Andes; the beautiful blue Indian orchid *Vanda caerulea*, brought to the verge of extinction by collectors; and so on. It is proper to draw attention to these rarities, but not to the exclusion of less glamorous but more useful plants and animals.

The Rare Breeds Survival Trust is a recently formed British organization with the objective of conserving breeds of domestic animals now

The remains of a ranch house in Africa's Great Rift Valley. Farmers cleared the forested slopes above the house for agriculture, thereby making them vulnerable to erosion. The first severe rains that fell buried the house in topsoil washed down from the deforested hillsides. Deforestation of hillsides was the kind of policy that denuded Crete and many Mediterranean countries. This picture vividly illustrates the processes that led to the collapse of Cretan agriculture and civilization—and that buried the palace at Knossos.

Young, wild cherry trees line a road near London's Gatwick Airport. Urban planning that allows for single-species stands of trees and beds of flowers makes poor provision for the varied needs of insects required for pollinating plants.

Governments create reserves to protect pretty rarities such as Primula scotia (above)—yet they permit the destruction of whole forests! Without forests, too little oxygen may be recycled to support advanced life forms on earth.

threatened with extinction. Until the oil crisis of the mid-1970s, few people in Britain's mechanized society thought seriously about the conservation of certain breeds of working horse. Attitudes have changed, though. Not long ago, an English farmer who had discarded his tractor and returned to horses explained why: "Instead of breaking down, needing spare parts, and depreciating in value, horses actually reproduce themselves, and their waste products can be used on the farm."

The interdependence of all forms of life on land—an interdependence that makes even the excrement of one kind of animal useful for other species, including man—is by no means a uniquely terrestrial situation. In this respect the sea is no different from the land. Just as air-breathing insects and invertebrates constitute a second stage after the photosynthesizing plants in the terrestrial food chain, so the copepods or krill provide a second stage in the marine environment after the phytoplankton (floating marine plant life). Just as little animals feed big animals

on land, so tiny krill feed great whales. As on land, too, there are areas of the oceans that are especially fertile; if we denude them, we are preparing an eventual disaster for ourselves; the sea's resources are by no means less limited than those on land.

A few years ago, in a spurt of technical expertise, the Danes found salmon feeding grounds in the Arctic and made the most of them. While the shelves in Danish fish stores temporarily groaned under the weight of salmon, the stock in Scottish rivers and lakes, and even those of North America, dwindled. In other words, to plunder one area may mean to deprive other areas as well. The Japanese are now netting the breeding grounds off the coast of east Africa. There can be only one long-term result of such policies. Marine life, like the forests on land, can be a renewable resource for mankind only if man himself manages the sea properly, with conservation in mind.

A few years ago, underwater fishing by individual sportsmen was a relatively uncommon

So the future for the Mediterranean looks bleak. But even the open Atlantic and North Sea are threatened. The oceans' fertile estuaries are already being destroyed by sewage, industrial effluent, and other kinds of pollution. The estuaries used to provide rich breeding grounds for the beginning of the marine food chain, for crustaceans, whitebait, and whiting. They were fertilized by the silt washed down from hills. Today they are poison. In the open waters, modern dragnet fishing tears at the seabed for fear of letting one fish escape, in a desperate search for profit. The effect on the ocean floor resembles that of taking a bulldozer through a field of growing wheat. The delicate balance of marine plants is so easily disturbed that re-covery takes a very long time. But there are also less obvious threats to the great expanses of the oceans, where exploitation of a prodigious and catastrophic nature is taking place, with a total disregard for breeding grounds or for interdependent food chains. The Peruvian anchovy, being fished almost to extinction, is an outstanding example of such disregard, because the anchovy is near the beginning of many food chains, and its extermination will mean starvation for other species, whose death will bring death to still others further along the chain.

The marine food chain can be considered in relatively simple terms. As on land, the sun's energy is captured by the photosynthesis of algae and other simple organisms. These are eaten by

The discovery of oil off Scotland has meant work and wealth for a hitherto neglected corner of the British Isles. But already sights such as this barge laying oil pipes near the Shetland Isles have brought doubts and fears to conservationists and all antipollution-minded citizens. Oil spills and leaks from pipes, pumps, and equipment—the inevitable paraphernalia of an oil find—can cause untold harm to the important wildlife of the area. Oil slicks will also add yet another burden to already heavily polluted offshore waters. These waters, and the estuarine and coastal waters, were once the richest in marine life: fish, shellfish, worms, and other animals. Now, as the polluted French estuary (right) shows, they are also the areas where pollution is most serious.

Below: divers collecting corals from the Great Barrier Reef off Australia. Research into the undersea environment is vital if we are to avoid turning vast areas of fertile ocean into watery desert. The sea is a source of valuable nutrient-rich fish and mollusks for man, and for his cattle and crops. Occasionally, though overexploitation, these marine harvests fail, and man must turn to already scarce land-based substitutes such as the protein-bearing soybean. Soybeans can be used to fatten cattle and for direct human consumption—under suitable disguises. Right: of the four kabobs here, the two on the left are made of soybean; the others are meat.

single-celled animals, which are preyed upon by larger, multicellular creatures. Still bigger animals are more selective or specialized feeders: mud-feeders such as plaice, mid-depth-feeders such as mackerel, and top-surface-feeders such as herring. Some species—the blue whale and the basking shark, for instance—live on plankton or microcrustaceans, despite their great size. Others eat small fish of many kinds. To take one example, the cod, at the end of a food chain, has probably eaten a great variety of smaller fry. If you over-fish the cod, the chances are that when you realize your mistake you can reverse the situation by waiting for young cod to mature before taking any more out of the water. Even if you had overfished them to extinction, you could simply forget about cod, promise not to do it again, and fall back on the next lower level of the food chain. But what if your fishing resulted in the extinction of a species that belongs at the beginning of a chain? Because higher species rely on that resource, its destruction would seriously threaten them, too. This is why the overfishing of the tiny anchovy off the coast of Peru is so reprehensible; it may mean the finish of an extensive food chain.

Imprudence at sea can mean trouble on land, because interdependence knows no limits to the complexity of interlocking relationships. Consider what happened in 1973, when the Peruvian anchovy catch dwindled to only about one tenth of the 1970 catch. By the 1970s, intensive animal husbandry in Europe and America had come to rely on fish meal from the anchovy as a feeding substance, and suddenly there was a short fall of many millions of tons of basic protein. The only available substitute was soybeans, mainly grown in the United States. Prices of the beans naturally rocketed, and speculators made fortunes. The United States was forced to curb exports of soybeans, particularly to Japan, and so the prices of other protein-rich cereals hit new all-time highs. Livestock feeds soared in price, affecting dairy, beef, pig, and poultry producers—and, of course, the consumer. The high cost of staple foods inevitably brought hardship to masses of poor people across the world.

Thus, human mismanagement of the marine environment led to human suffering on land by virtually destroying a resource that only 30 years earlier had been heralded as a great under-exploited food source, a splendid answer to the problem of world shortage. This kind of mistake makes us realize how little we know about basic ecology, about the interdependence of free-living systems. There is no more dangerous assumption than the assumption that if we exploit our resources to the limit, we shall adapt to new situations or find new resources, as man has always done. The truth of the matter is plain: man has never adapted; he has moved. But now we have nowhere to go.

Endangered Mammals

All mammals are under threat of extinction. Man is the greatest threat to all species, including himself; indeed, it is man who, directly or indirectly, has been the principal cause of the extinction of animal species in recent times. The blue-green algae, long ages ago, threatened their own existence by polluting the atmosphere with oxygen and were thus the direct cause of their own downfall. The giant dinosaurs apparently ate so much that they destroyed their habitat, and caused the extinction of many plants and animal species. Today it is man whose greediness may be having a similar effect.

Primitive man was already a great hunter of wildlife. The Pleistocene period, which began some 600,000 years ago, was characterized by fluctuating cold and mild climates throughout the world. Although there were periods of glaciation, the large mammals that had evolved in the Pliocene period were successfully adapted to such changes. Rhinoceroses, for example, were able to thrive in tundra conditions where the subsoil was frozen throughout the year. Everywhere, in fact, the Pleistocene was dominated by highly adapted and very large land animals. North America had huge elephants, bison almost half as big again as our contemporary species, and even oversize lions. In South America there were giant armadillos and ground sloths; Australasia had 12-foot-tall birds and giant marsupials; Madagascar had an elephant bird that weighed half a ton; hippopotamuses throve in Europe, together with a great variety of other highly adaptable big mammals. When excavations were carried out in Trafalgar Square in the very heart of London in 1962, the fossilized bones and teeth of a hippopotamus and a lion were discovered— proof that only a few thousand years ago such animals flourished there. Great herds of mammoths roamed across Asia and Russia, and probably in eastern Europe, and huge saber-toothed tigers preyed upon the larger of the diverse

This painting of a European bison from a cave at Altamira, Spain, was made by a cave-dweller of the Pleistocene period. The Stone Age hunters of the Pleistocene were probably largely responsible for the extinction of many of the big land animal species that had roamed over much of the world.

60

ungulate species (large herbivorous mammals).

The best fossil record of the Pleistocene fauna of North America was found, some years ago, in the asphalt tar pits of Los Angeles, where 50-odd mammalian species were evidently resident up to about 4500 years ago. Nearly half of them are now extinct. The gigantic short-faced bear is gone, and so also are the Columbian mammoths and such huge soaring birds of prey as *Teratornis incredibilis*, which had a wingspan of some 17 feet. The California condor is of special interest because it is still with us, but there are possibly only a few dozen left. What is clear from the tar-pit fossil record is that the major loss of the great Pleistocene fauna dates back roughly to the time of the coming of man in large numbers.

Today the only elephants in North America are in zoos. The sole remaining hint of the grandeur of Pleistocene fauna is to be found in Africa. Even there, though, the speed of the decline of many mammal species is not appreciated by most observers. Fossil history tells us quite a lot about the destruction of wildlife by the "killer ape" (to give humanity its most cruel name) as his skills and reproductive performance and numbers were increased by the plentiful supply of animal victims. Yet wildlife eventually won a reprieve when man began to domesticate food-producing animals. This development was probably stimulated by the reduction in availability of the huge wild animals, and it took pressure off the wild resources. Somehow, though, the pressure never entirely let up; hunting was a natural human activity. The Europeans who arrived in New Zealand following Captain Cook's first voyage in 1769 exterminated 14 species—a tiny example of a process that has continued on a worldwide scale all through the ages.

If you read accounts of travelers and hunters such as "Karamoja" Bell or naturalists such as Jackson, Percival, or Theodore Roosevelt, who all visited Africa in the years between 1880 and

The elephants (above) and the California condor (left), from a painting made in 1838 by the ornithologist John James Audubon, are survivors—the condor only just—of the Pleistocene overkill. From fossil evidence we know that in America alone nearly half of the 50 or so mammalian species known to have flourished there are now extinct. Hunting and habitat destruction are the most powerful means by which man has brought about the extinction of the greater part of the world's vanished fauna.

1920, you will discover that they are talking about a very different Africa from the continent we know today. Karamoja Bell (who got his nickname from hunting in Karamoja, Uganda) describes how he camped at Namalu, a village in Uganda that now consists of a prison farm and a small row of shops, including a post office, and he expresses his wonder at the wealth of game animals, especially zebra, topi, eland, and oryx. He himself was seeking ivory, and made a fortune from shooting elephants with a small-caliber rifle, a 0.275 Rigby, which few modern hunters would dream of using against the big beasts (in fact, it is now illegal to shoot at elephants with anything less than a 0.375-caliber rifle). In the published account of his visit to Namalu at the end of the 19th century, he also tells of rising early in the morning, taking a few paces from his tent on the outskirts of the village, and shooting one of the throngs of antelope that were unconcernedly grazing nearby.

At that same spot today—in the heart of a game sanctuary, and still, indeed, one of the

Below: illustration from Sir William Cornwallis Harris's Wild Sports of Africa. *Big-game hunting once had an enormous romantic appeal for many people and was a favorite subject with writers and movie-producers. Originally man killed for food and only later did he kill for pleasure, and for the trophy industry. Large-scale killing together with destruction of habitats, has reduced whole species of African wildlife to danger levels.*

richest wildlife areas of Uganda—some game animals can be seen, but no one would describe the place as teeming with wild beasts. Great excitement greets the spotting of an oribi, a Jackson's hartebeest, or a warthog. Zebras can be seen in small groups of 10 or 20, but it is very rare to see a large herd. If the eland see a human being, they start to run at a seemingly gentle pace; but they hold their heads in the air with grim determination, and even a motor vehicle has trouble keeping pace with them. They trot on for great distances without stopping, without glancing back, and with only one apparent objective: to put as much distance between the danger and themselves as possible. Any vehicle spells danger; any man spells danger; and they run.

The contrast of such scenes with the picture of Karamoja Bell strolling out of his tent to shoot his breakfast is dramatic. Some will say that the Africa of Bell's time is far in the past, that we are now more enlightened, and that changes of this sort are no longer in evidence, but that is not

Above: the setting sun over Tsavo National Park glints on the waterholes, which at this time of day should be thronged with drinking animals. The emptiness of the scene is perhaps a grim pointer to the future for wildlife in this once-teeming continent.

true. In 1961 a pharmacologist friend and I climbed down a 2000-foot escarpment on the Rift Valley to a flat area separated from the rest of Uganda by this escarpment, and from the rest of Africa by what was then called Lake Albert (since renamed Lake Mobutu). We wanted to find a site where animals were abundant in order to study nutrition and anesthetization techniques by dart gun, and these 90 square miles— the Tonia–Kaiso flats—looked good on the map. They *were* good; we were rewarded beyond our most optimistic dreams. The whole place was like a wildlife farm, alive with kongoni, kob, warthogs, waterbucks, duikers, brooding buffaloes, and lions. Monkeys and baboons scrambled over the escarpment, and we came across an assortment of snakes, too. When we climbed down the steep slope, we could see the open spaces burning with the rich, brown-red movement of kob. As we walked across the floor of the flats, the animals would simply stand up as we approached, wag their tails, stamp their feet, move about a bit, and stare inquisitively. We had suddenly come face to face with the reality of the Pleistocene: just two of us and thousands upon thousands of timid but unfrightened animals.

We visited the flats on several occasions for about four years. Then, suddenly, the situation changed. Poachers, having exhausted other regions, had at last discovered an area that had been protected until now because people had mostly done their killing from the comfort of a vehicle that could not climb the escarpment. Now the poachers had burned the grass, knowing that the animals would congregate to eat the fresh green shoots that sprout up on the first rain, and then they made their killing. It took just six months of sporadic shooting to make a drastic change in the character of the animal population. By 1970 most of the poachers had left or been forced out of Uganda, but the harm was done. The shooting and the fear had broken up breeding groups. The wildlife of the Tonia–Kaiso flats was almost exterminated; animals were so scarce that it was no longer worth visiting the area for study purposes. The vegetation,

too, had been severely damaged by the burning.

Noel Simon, of the International Union for the Conservation of Nature, tells much the same story. In his book *Between the Sunlight and the Thunder,* he writes about great herds that inhabited the Rift Valley as recently as 1942, when he first drove from Kijobe to Nakuru in Kenya. Five years later, they had dwindled. Today, only a few animals are likely to be found there.

Some areas do recover, of course, but the main trend is toward collapse—collapse brought on by man's greed and ruthlessness. Yet we have long known that this is so. Noel Simon quotes a concerned observer of the African scene who, in 1894, said: "It would be melancholy to think that such glorious creatures as the eland, the kudu, the sable antelope, and the zebra were passing into extinction when they might be saved and perpetuated by our making a little effort in the right direction." Since then, a "little effort" has indeed been made. Forced to recognize the excessive destruction of wildlife for fun and profit, authorities have passed game laws, and have set up sanctuaries or national parks in an attempt to stem the destructive tide. But it often seems to be a question of too little and too late.

The testimony of the thousands of ivory tusks below 10 pounds in weight tells us that already in the 1890s people were killing very young

Mixed grasses, sedges, and herbs form a protective mat helping to bind soil particles together, retain moisture, and thus prevent erosion. Repeated burning of the grass, to encourage growth of the tender young shoots to feed cattle, eliminates most of the plant species and eventually exposes topsoil and grass roots, leading to erosion.

Right: a lake in the extinct Ngorongoro Crater in Tanzania. The whole crater area is now a protected reserve and a haven for many animals and birds.

elephants in their eagerness for ivory. Today colobus monkeys in Ethiopia are being pursued for their beautiful black-and-white pelts. The beauty of the leopard's skin similarly threatens its survival. And the white rhinoceros is already extinct in many parts of Africa where it used to be abundant; its horn is prized as an alleged aphrodisiac in the Orient, where people will pay anything from $50 to $200 for an ounce of horn powder. A single white-rhino horn can weigh between 10 and 20 pounds, and thus there is much profit to be gained from killing the gentle creatures. The white rhino lives in high-rainfall zones where the grass is tall and the bush is thick; this, combined with their gentleness, makes it easy to stalk and kill these splendid mammals, which are being destroyed not for food or clothing but to stimulate the failing sexual ability of elderly degenerates. Nature is sacrificed to human vanity or greed.

Take, for another example, the assumption that domestic animals are intrinsically more important than wildlife. Near Nairobi in Kenya

Above: the black-and-white colobus monkey is an inhabitant of high treetops in Ethiopia and feeds almost exclusively on leaves. The pet trade, medical research, and the clearance of their forest habitat are a serious threat to the survival of many species of monkey. The colobus is hunted for its strikingly patterned fur.

Left: the African white, or square-lipped, rhino is the biggest of the world's five species of rhino. All suffer from human poachers who kill them for their horns. The horns—really agglutinated hair—have a reputation in parts of Eastern Asia for supposed near-magical medical properties, although research has failed to find any curative properties in them.

lies the district of Kajiado, where live the Masai, a tribe of tall, fine people who pride themselves on the ownership of cattle. Like a Western businessman with his portfolio of securities, the Masai is proud of his fortune, although it is not the amount of money he owns, but the number of his cattle, that counts for him. He does not care whether the cattle are weak, emaciated, or tick-infested: what matters is the number. Many tribes in Africa have a similar attitude. The Karamajong will go to war over cattle. Their chiefs will fix the price for a bride by the number of cattle required to surround her and hide her legs from view.

Traditionally the Masai are nomadic. They settle for a while in one area until their cattle and goats have eaten most of the vegetation; then they move on to new pastures. The Masai can accumulate sums of money that make them relatively wealthy. It is virtually impossible to tax nomadic people. The Kenyan authorities felt that it would be a good idea to encourage the Masai to live a more settled existence. The district of Kajiado was chosen as an experiment.

Overleaf: Masai herdsmen from the Kenya-Tanzania border area with their cattle. Unlike those of most nomadic peoples who have domesticated animals native to their areas, these cattle were introduced into Africa from Asia about 4000 years ago. As well as supplying blood—small amounts are drawn from cows through a tiny incision made in the jugular vein—and milk for food, Masai cattle are a source of riches and prestige to their owners, who tolerate no rivalry from grazing wildlife.

Kajiado lies between the Nairobi and Amboseli national parks, and serves these areas with a hinterland for the migration of wildlife; the conservation laws of Kenya prohibit the killing of wild animals without purchasing a licence. The Masai needed some form of protection, however, and they were permitted to kill wildlife if they or their cattle were threatened. This means that the Masai warrior is within the law if, having killed a wild animal, he merely claims that the beast was eating the grass needed for his cows. The zebra was the first species to vanish from Kajiado, although the zebra's careful selection of grasses offered little competition to cattle. As Kajiado acts as a reservoir for the Amboseli and Nairobi national parks, the slaughter in this district could eventually destroy the wildlife of both these important parks.

Zebra skins can fetch as much as $500, and the skins of smaller animals, such as Thomson's gazelle and ostrich, are much sought after for handbags and purses. The Masai can use the money they get from such pillage to buy more and more cattle. But, there is a law in Kenya

Left: a taxidermist's well-stocked studio in Nairobi, Kenya. The conservation laws in Kenya are meant to restrict the killing of wildlife, but some culling of animals from restricted habitats will probably be to the advantage of the species. With the demands for trophies from a thriving tourist industry, however, conservation laws are often flouted.

abroad. The effectiveness of any law depends on the ability to police it, the recognition of its value by law-abiding members of the community, and the enthusiasm for enforcement. In Tibet the giant panda is recognized to be of such value that the killing of one is punishable by death.

In Kenya conservation laws do exist, and the offenders can at least be exposed and brought to justice if public pressure is sufficiently great; but in many other countries the wildlife is without any legal protection at all. We can all play a part by pressing our governments to assist developing countries with education about the economic value of wildlife and about resource management. We can also bring pressure to bear to prohibit the importation and trade in live animals, skins, elephant ivory, and other products of rare species. Effective legislation already exists in the USA (which has led in this type of action), in Britain, and in a few other countries, but there are often loopholes in the laws, and many governments simply do not bother about such matters.

To someone who is not familiar with African wildlife the scene in certain areas of that great continent looks dazzling, with a marvelous abundance of wild creatures. In reality, one sees a pitiful remnant of what was once a spectacle of unrivaled beauty. To the casual tourist, the sight of giraffes striding across the great plains of Serengeti in Tanzania seems to represent the ultimate in natural grace and rhythm. To the biologist, though, it is a representation of tragedy! Giraffes evolved to stretch up into trees and take their food from parts of the plant that no other animal could reach. To see these tall creatures standing head and shoulders above the tallest vegetation can only mean environmental degeneracy. Man has cut down the high trees, thus depriving the giraffe of its natural habitat.

When giraffes normally browse on trees, they encourage the umbrella shape by eating the underside. Trees trimmed in this way provide shade and shelter for small plants and animals. In the Nairobi National Park, many trees are not umbrella-shaped but pear-shaped, because the giraffes have to bend down and trim them from

that should prevent this misuse of wildlife. No skins may be sold without a certificate, and any visitor to East Africa should insist on obtaining a certificate if purchasing any skin or article made from a wild animal. Many conservationists wish to ban the sale of all trophies and skins of wild animals, yet the revenue earned from such articles provides one valid reason for the conservation of this natural resource. On the whole this type of law has worked quite well, but today bribery and corruption are openly talked of in Nairobi as ways of selling illegal ivory and skins

Giraffes, which are found from the Sudan to South Africa, prefer savanna and bush country to forests. Their main diet is the upper foliage of the thorny acacia trees that grow to a height of 30 feet and—because of the way they are constantly pruned by giraffes—are normally umbrella-shaped. Over large areas of the African savanna, man has cut down these tall trees, forcing giraffes to bend down and browse from the tops of smaller trees. Thus, the pear-shaped trees (left) are now a more familiar sight in East Africa, for instance, and the stooping giraffe (right) has become a symbol of the way man is altering the wilderness to suit himself, with little thought for the wildlife whose habitat it is.

above. This indicates that the natural ecosystem that once supported and encouraged the upward evolution of such species is already in a severe state of decline. And the giraffe is merely one example of the general deterioration. Just as small-scale habitat destruction annihilates insects, and the annihilation of insects in turn lessens plant and bird diversity, so also the large-scale habitat destruction that man has inflicted upon the world and its oceans is destroying the residual large mammals. Not one of the large wild-animal species is safe.

To the agriculturalist grassland is a splendid achievement; but to the biologist it is degenerate. Fence off any area of land, and exclude animal life, and it will quickly be colonized by bushes and trees. To the agriculturalist this is a mess; but to the biologist it is the diversity upon which evolution and life depend. Indeed, the agriculturalist himself depends on diversity, for his efforts produce not only wheat, but corn, fruits, nuts, beans, peas, cabbage, pigs, hens, sheep, eggs, and milk. It is true that the best way for the farmer to grow and harvest crops is through monoculture, but, taken as a whole, diversity is still there—not in a single field, but perhaps, in the entire farm.

If we look at Africa today, however, we see a vast wilderness racing toward monoculture. The stooping giraffes stand as a symbol of what is happening: a continent that once taught animals to reach high into the trees for sustenance now forces them to bend low in their search for food. One of the most enlightening studies of the effects of African monoculture related to the elephant, and was made a few years ago by biologists working in eastern Africa, supported by laboratory facilities in London. After man himself, the elephant has actually had the greatest impact on African habitats. Its power to influence vegetation on a massive scale is due to two of its characteristics: size and longevity. The size and long life of the elephant pose a real conservation problem in modern Africa, for two reasons. First, the remaining habitats to which elephants are confined are, as we shall see, largely unsuitable. Secondly, the impact of the elephant on these habitats is such that it endangers the existence of other species, particularly those with stringent habitat requirements.

When the East African National Parks were formed earlier in our own century, the major objective was conservation of the last great remains of the world's natural wildlife heritage. But the objective was not only to conserve but also to display. This meant that people had to

see the animals. A rinderpest epidemic had killed off much of the domestic livestock of eastern Africa at the turn of the century, and that fact, combined with the depredations of the tsetse fly, meant that large areas of land supported only small cattle populations but were rich in wildlife, which could tolerate the tsetse fly and trypanosomes. These areas appeared eminently suitable for national parks, because they had formerly been used for cattle and were therefore relatively open, with much grassland. This seemed a splendid location for the easy viewing of animals.

The entire parkland region, which includes the Kabelega (previously Murchison Falls) National Park, comprises an area of close to 1 million acres. The Nile flows across it on its journey to the Mediterranean, and to the north of the river there is a zone of close-canopy woodland, which thins out into open woods and then grassland savanna. To the north of the park, along the course of the Nile, there remains some high forest, the Zoka Forest, and this was earmarked as an elephant sanctuary. To the south of the Nile there is no close-canopy woodland; but farther to the south of the vast park area, another high forest, the Budongo, stretches for about 160 square miles.

In times past, elephants had been accustomed

to migrating along the attractive, well-watered course of the Nile to the Zoka Forest in the north, southward through Budongo to the Ruwenzori Mountains, and eastward to Mount Elgon and its high woodlands. Growing human populations, however, had gradually encroached on wildlife territory and had ultimately severed the migration routes. If a herd of elephants marched through a farm or garden, the proprietors—quite naturally—either shot them or requested the Game Department to do so. The human thirst for ivory and profit also added to the dangers of elephant life outside what finally became national-park boundaries. So at last the herds congregated by the thousand in the relative safety of the parks. What might have seemed their salvation, though, was fraught with danger for both the habitat and the elephants themselves. The build-up of great herds of long-living creatures with voracious appetites in an area hemmed in by human settlements resulted in spectacular damage to the park vegetation: the trees were rapidly eaten and debarked, and their loss soon posed a threat to the continued existence of the hungry elephants.

In a study of population dynamics which commenced in 1960 and was published in 1968, Dr. Richard Laws, a director of the Nuffield Institute

of Tropical Animal Ecology in Uganda, produced evidence in support of the rather startling idea that the self-regulatory mechanisms that may have been adequate in the past for maintaining elephant populations in balance would not operate in the confines of a national park, because the increasing population was progressively destroying its own habitat. As a result, elephant health was being undermined, calving intervals were losing their normal rhythm, longevity was being reduced, and the general condition of the animals was visibly deteriorating. On the basis of what he and his colleagues had seen of the growing distortion of population dynamics, Laws predicted that the rise in numbers, destruction of resources, and degeneration of health would bring on a total collapse of the elephants—in other words, virtual extinction—before the end of the century.

Laboratory support for Dr. Laws's contention came from Dr. Sylvia Sikes and Mr. Richard Fiennes of the Nuffield Institute of Comparative Medicine in London; their pathological studies indicated that the elephants in the East African National Parks were affected by a severe calcification of the arteries, not unlike hardening of the arteries in human beings. They were also suffering from a high incidence of abscesses in the jaw. The London pathologists were able to show that these defects were found only in elephants confined to the parks, which, having destroyed the woodland, were being forced to eat only grass. The average amount of diseased area in the aorta (the principal large artery in the body) of middle-aged grassland elephants was an incredibly high 44.5 per cent of the total area, as against less than 0.3 per cent of calcification among elephants in the same age group that had lived in the remaining natural woodland regions of eastern Africa.

Further evidence that the cause of these differences was entirely nutritional came from the British and also American laboratories. There can be no doubt that grassland simply cannot provide the diversity and quantity of essential nutrients available in woodland, with its high-nutrient leaves, its large, oil-rich seeds, and its fibrous bark and woody vegetation. Prior to the studies of Dr. Laws and his British co-workers, studies carried out by American scientists had already revealed that elephants would naturally have some 90 per cent of their stomach contents as browse material. In the parks where the elephants had eaten most of the trees to death, the Laws study found that grass made up roughly 70 to 80 per cent of their stomach contents.

In order to conserve the elephant population of the East African National Parks, it became necessary to impose some external control on their numbers, and this meant shooting isolated families of them—so as not to disturb the whole population—for the survival of the species. The cropping of elephants provided the Africans with tons of food, skins, and a significant amount

Left: elephant poachers and, right, recovered spoils. A few years ago ivory was fetching between $2–$3 per pound. Since then it has rocketed to $50 a pound. The beleaguered Asian communities in parts of Africa used ivory as a means of exporting wealth; corrupt Africans used ivory as a means of gaining illegal fortunes; and the Japanese recognized that the extermination of elephants would increase the price of ivory, making it a good hedge against inflation. Although the Asians have been forced out, and the Japanese are showing less interest, ivory sales still continue at near-record prices. Frequently, more than 50 per cent of the tusks sold weigh less than 10 pounds each, showing that very young elephants are being killed. Without a policy of careful management, the policing of wild populations, and rational utilization and breeding for their ivory, meat and skin, the future for the greatest of the land mammals is indeed black.

published, the United States was sending out around 700 whaling vessels (which were small by today's standards), and Melville in his famous novel was already clearly asking the conservationist question: "The whale ships, now penetrating even through Behring's straits, and to the remotest secret drawers and lockers of the world; and the thousand harpoons and lances darted along all continental coasts; the moot point is, whether Leviathan can long endure so wide a chase, and so remorseless a havoc; whether he must not at last be exterminated from the waters and the last whale, like the last man, smoke his last pipe, and then himself evaporate in the final puff."

No really positive step toward whale conservation was taken until December 1946, when an International Whaling Commission was created to secure the protection of some of the smaller stocks of whales in the North Atlantic. The commission had little impact. It managed eventually to establish a quota system, but every such system was easily sidestepped by those who chose to do so. In the 1950s, conservationists argued for a moratorium on all killing—a cessation of whaling for 10 years—but by 1962 it became clear that Japan, the Netherlands, Norway, and Russia would not agree to the imposition of strict quotas, let alone a full-scale moratorium. At that time the New York Zoological

10-year moratorium on killings, but a motion to this effect at the London meeting failed to win the necessary two-thirds majority of International Whaling Commission votes. In 1975 the Commission finally legislated complete protection of all whales except the sperm whale; but, as Richard Fitter, the Honorary Secretary of the Fauna Preservation Society, commented afterward, "All they did was to place on record the species they had brought to the verge of extinction, and which were no longer worth chasing. It was a black page in human history."

At best, even when agreements to limit whale fishing have been reached, they have been ignored by certain nations, among them the Japanese and the Russians. Unfortunately, police control is totally lacking. Yet the only way to save the whales now is to enforce a prohibition of all killings in order to allow stocks to build up while we try to gain the scientific knowledge we need to keep these great creatures with us. Without a conservation program of this nature, they face extinction in a few years.

The United States deserves credit for having injected a ray of hope into the gloomy picture as long ago as 1971, when, out of patience with the delaying tactics of more short-sighted nations, it placed most commercial whale species on its Endangered Species List; this means that no part of the animal can be legally imported into the USA. But so far the example America set has not been followed by the nations whose whaling activities are most in need of being curbed.

Like the elephant and the whale, the tiger of India has been brought to the verge of extermination in recent years. Although barely 1000 tigers remain in the subcontinent, as compared with 100,000 only 50 or 60 years ago, the picture here is somewhat brighter. Recently the World Wildlife Fund—an organization set up in 1961 for the purpose of collecting money and spending it on conservation—launched a campaign that it calls "Operation Tiger." The Fund estimates that it needs about $7½ million to save the tiger, and it has managed to raise this sum. Meanwhile, the exportation of tiger skins has been prohibited by the Indian government, and their importation

Society began to sponsor work on whale breeding habits; among other things, the society set up a scientific observation post on the Island of Valdez, off the coast of Argentina, where the right whale has its breeding grounds. There was strong opposition among whalers even to such objective fact-gathering.

By 1973 the whale had become a subject of world concern. In June, when the International Whaling Commission gathered in London for one of its periodical meetings, the London *Times* marked the occasion by printing a half-page picture of a blue whale, captioned: "One is killed every 20 minutes." The Stockholm Environmental Conference of 1972 had already called for a

has also been banned by America, Britain, and other governments. The Indian Wildlife Protection Act of 1972 has made it illegal to hunt tigers as well as 41 other endangered species. And there is no longer any profit to be made from the sale of tiger skins, for even if a tiger has to be shot because of threat to human life, every part of the animal becomes government property.

But the list of endangered species is long, and one ray of sunlight is hardly enough to make conservation-minded people happy. An organization named the International Union for the Conservation of Nature (IUCN) is dedicated to promoting and supporting any action that helps to perpetuate wild nature and resources all over the world, and one of its functions is to collect data on, and maintain lists of, wild animals and plants in danger of extinction. Its authoritative list, known as the *Red Data Book*, is kept up to date and published periodically in loose-leaf form. The "Red" in *Red Data Book* stands, of course, for danger, but the IUCN also compiles another list, which might appropriately be called the *Black Book*: a record of species that have passed into extinction since the year 1600, when adequate descriptions of living organisms began to be made. According to the list, in 1600 there existed 4226 species of mammals; since then, 36 have become extinct, and at least 120 are close to extinction. In 1600, there appear to have been 8684 species of birds; since then, 94 have become extinct, and 187 are in danger of extinction.

Richard Fitter—the spokesman for the Fauna Preservation Society, whose wry comment on the 1975 meeting of the International Whaling Commission I have already quoted—has selected what he considers to be the top 25 of the most endangered mammals listed in the *Red Data Book*. His selection does not include elephants and whales because he seems to be slightly more optimistic about their future than I am. His "top" choices are, in his words, "seemingly hopeless cases where we know (or think we do) just what needs to be done, but for economic, financial, political, social, or cultural reasons cannot at present see our way to do it. And this pinpoints the real reason why these animals are becoming extinct: that for the most part man does not care enough whether they do or not." Let us briefly run through the Fitter list:

(1) The aye-aye, found in Malagasy, is the sole surviving representative of a whole primate family, the Daubentoniidae. Not more than perhaps 50 of these relatives of the lemur are left.

The mountain gorilla, found only in mountainous parts of Uganda, Zaïre, and Rwanda, is the largest of the apes. Gorillas fetch high prices on the international zoo market, which—allied to the fact that, even without man's intervention, some 50 per cent of the young die through accidents or disease—has ensured that these animals are now fast dwindling in number.

Local superstition has it that it is bad luck to see an aye-aye, and they are slaughtered indiscriminately. To be effective, any rescue attempt must be made very soon.

(2) The population of golden lion marmosets has diminished to between 400 and 600, which live near Rio de Janeiro in Brazil. The pet trade and deforestation are responsible for their plight, but there *is* some hope here. They are about the smallest of the primates, and hence of value to medical research; and so they might be saved by breeding in the laboratories of drug firms or research institutions.

(3) The pig-tailed langur is confined to the Mentawai Islands of West Sumatra. Again deforestation and hunting constitute the threat. These animals have never been kept in any zoo, and few attempts have been made to save them from extinction.

(4) The mountain gorilla must rate high on anyone's list of endangered primates. Fewer than 1000 remain in volcanic regions of Rwanda, Uganda, and Zaïre, and the population is decreasing rapidly. Mountain gorillas are highly valued by zoos. In 1964, I saw 16 babies being transported through Uganda on their way to Europe; some were destined to live in solitary confinement because the price was so high that few zoos could buy more than one. At that time I had no idea of the plight of these mammals, and I assumed that

The giant otter inhabits rivers in the northern part of South America. It is another victim of the fur-hunters and trophy-seekers, its pelt fetching a price as high as that of a jaguar. Although the International Fur Trade Federation has been operating a voluntary ban on its fur since the early 1970s, nothing short of total protection can save this attractive animal from extinction.

there must be many thousands if such a haul of baby gorillas could be made. Later I learned that the technique of capturing the babies involves shooting and killing the parents.

(5) Red wolves are seriously threatened despite active conservation measures of the US Fish and Wildlife Service. They are confined to part of the coastal marshlands of Texas and Louisiana, where only one or two pure populations are known to survive. Human beings normally hate all wolves, and hunters are quick to kill this outstanding species.

(6) The Mexican grizzly bear may already be extinct; the last firmly recorded population was destroyed by a rancher more than 10 years ago.

(7) Black-footed ferrets apparently live only in South Dakota. They are dying out because they are being killed by poisons meant for prairie dogs, which farmers look upon as pests.

(8) The giant otter can be saved from early extinction by nothing short of total prohibition of the Amazonian animal trade.

(9) The Florida cougar lives in the Everglades National Park, where it could be saved by vigorous conservation methods. Outside the park, unfortunately, farmers kill it on sight.

(10) The Asiatic lion has already received attention from official wildlife-conservation bodies, which have established reserves and sanctuaries. Its numbers continue to decline, however, be-

Above: the Asiatic, or Indian, lion. Asiatic lions are restricted to the Gir Forest northwest of Bombay, and have suffered because of encroachment by agriculture on their hunting territory.

The Mediterranean monk seal (below) has been dispossessed of its breeding sites by human vacationers.

cause overgrazing destroys its habitat, thus robbing it of its prey.

(11) As I have indicated, the tiger is near the end of its days unless the conjoint efforts of the World Wildlife Fund and the Indian Government are successful. It may perhaps have a reprieve of sorts by living on for a while in zoos.

(12) The Japanese sea lion is probably already extinct by now. A few used to be seen off the Korean coast, but none has been sighted recently.

(13) Mediterranean monk seals have been robbed of their breeding caves by vacationists. They are not protected by law, and no breeding colony lies within any nature reserve.

(14) The South American manatee has been ruthlessly hunted for its fine meat, and this has brought it nearer to extinction than any other Amazonian mammal. Its extermination would be a great loss, for it grazes on water plants, occupying a niche that is not duplicated by other aquatic animals, and helps to keep water conditions in a manageable state; without manatees, the many varieties of waterweeds take over and life in the water rapidly deteriorates.

(15) Przewalski's horses survive in the wild

Above: the Florida manatee, the most northerly of the sea cow species. Manatees are all animals of shallow coastal waters and large rivers. The Florida manatee is effectively protected and its numbers increasing. Not so the South American species, which is seriously threatened by hunting: its meat is regarded as a great delicacy, and the creatures are easily netted.

only on the Mongolian-Chinese border, where there are perhaps 50. They have been successfully reared in Western zoos, but this does not assure their survival as a wildlife species.

(16) The remaining great Indian rhinoceroses live mostly in Nepal. They are poached for the allegedly aphrodisiac properties of the horn. More antipoaching patrols might help, but only a few hundred of these great beasts, which look as though they are armor-plated, are likely to survive at best. In a similarly critical state are its near relations the Sumatran rhino (17) and the northern white rhino (18).

(19) Formosan sika deer have been hunted to virtual extinction, and the only hope rests in the existence of a small captive herd farmed for meat.

(20) Manipur brow-antlered deer are confined to a small sanctuary in India—a "sanctuary," however, that is heavily poached. Fitter suggests that turning the area into a national park might save this particular species.

(21) The tamarau of the Philippines has the hair of a goat and the head of a cow, and its meat is so tasty that hunters have brought it to the verge of extinction.

(22) The kouprey, like the tamarau, is being eaten to death. It has the misfortune to live in war-ravaged Cambodia, where, quite possibly, the last remaining animals have already found their way into hungry stomachs.

(23) The Arabian oryx, according to Fitter, is a prime example of an animal brought near to

The plains on the Sino-Mongolian border are the home of the last true wild horse, Przewalski's horse (a mare and foal are pictured above). The species, which is smaller than the domestic horse, is now rare in the wild, with a recent sighting estimating a total of about 50. There are several specimens in European zoos, however, and these have bred successfully.

extinction by human predation. Continuously chased on horseback and camelback, and finally with four-wheel-drive vehicles, it is by now almost certainly extinct in the wild. Fortunately, a few of the animals have been rescued from the desert, and breeding herds have been established at Phoenix, Arizona, in Qatar, and at the Los Angeles Zoo. This situation is not unlike that of the Père David's deer, which were exterminated in China during the Boxer Rebellion of 1900. A few were rescued and taken to England, where they bred well; they are now supplying nucleus breeding herds to repopulate their original habitat in China. Possibly the Arabian oryx will someday be returned to the desert.

(24) The dibatag gazelle and (25) the walia ibex are both indigenous to mountain regions of Somalia and Ethiopia. Although living in habitats not easily accessible to human beings, they have been sought out and killed for food. Few, if any, of them now survive.

A fact that must strike many who examine Richard Fitter's list is that they are a collection of lost causes; it may be that the tiger will be saved at the last minute. If it is saved, it will only be as the result of immense efforts by all the different conservation groups.

The single-horned Indian rhinoceros, like its African relatives, owes its rarity largely to horn-hunters but also to the fact that it produces only one calf every three years.

The now extremely rare Manipur brow-antlered deer, whose habitat, and last refuge, is the floating mat of vegetation on the Logtak Lake Sanctuary in Manipur, India.

Everyone has heard of the plight of the tiger and the whale and there is a common concern about these species. Yet, by contrast, how many people have heard of the pig-tailed langur, or know about or even care about its plight? The *Red Data Book* confronts us with many endangered species that really very few people even know about, let alone care about.

The three conclusions that can be drawn from the discussion are: first, the list of endangered species has an important message for conservation. We can single out a few rare species on which to focus attention but the underlying truth is that all large animal species are threatened.

Secondly, the television and tourist image of wildlife is dangerously misleading. It is the isolated pockets rich in wildlife that the tourists are taken to and films made about, whilst the trauma that exists outside the boundaries of that vision is not seen. To make a good film it is only natural to piece together the best animal shots to give the impression of a wealth of nature. It is only good business for the tour operators to take people to centers of high animal density. Regrettably, this gives people a misleading impression that what they see is representative of the whole of that region's wildlife.

Thirdly, it is also clear that habitat destruction poses the biggest threat to wildlife. There is little point in striving to conserve the remaining pocket of, say, the red-throated hartebeests in Loitokitok if the whole environment on which the species depends is collapsing. Laws can perhaps stem the destruction but no law can bring high trees immediately back to Africa's giraffes once man has cut them down. In the next chapter we shall examine some of the far-reaching implications of habitat destruction.

In 1961 the plight of the Arabian oryx was such that its only hope of survival lay in capturing a sufficient number of the animals to form a small herd for breeding in captivity. The Fauna Preservation Society, assisted by the World Wildlife Fund, organized Operation Oryx to save the Arabian oryx by capture. The spur to action came early in 1961 when a motorized raiding party from Qatar crossed the forbidding Rub-al-Khali and having traveled about 500 miles to the north killed at least 48 oryx—about half the remaining known population. The area of desert where the oryx were to be found covered some 8000 square miles. The rescue operation was mounted under the leadership of Major Ian Grimwood, at that time Chief Game Warden of Kenya. Whilst preparations were going on, it was learned that the hunting party from Qatar, having located the remaining herd, had again returned to the area. And when Major Grimwood's train arrived there, the Operation Oryx team estimated that only 11 animals had escaped the raiders' guns. Only four of these were caught but so much attention had been focused on the plight of the Arabian oryx that the few zoos with one or two specimens immediately transferred these to Phoenix, Arizona, where they formed the nucleus herd of Arabian oryx. Six governments, five zoos and many conservation societies contributed in one way or another to the build-up of the "world herd." Today, the number of Arabian oryx stands at about 106 in captivity and this number is divided between different zoos as a precaution against any natural disaster—disease, say—wiping out the whole herd. Operation Oryx is a typical example of how wildlife may ultimately find a home only in captivity. It is also a clear message to those who run zoos. At one time zoos themselves constituted a threat to wildlife because of the number killed in capture, transit, and the very high mortality rate among the newborn or even failure to breed in captivity. To play their role in conservation zoos must become centers for the breeding of rare species.

Disaster
in the Desert

The greatest of the conservation issues is habitat destruction, and nowhere has attention been focused more dramatically on this process than in the Sahel, an immense area stretching all the way across northern Africa, within which the desert is marching inexorably southward. For the past two decades, recurrent long periods of drought in the region have meant crop failures, dead and dying cattle, and famine. The desert of the Sahara is expanding at the rate of about one and a half miles a year.

In earlier chapters of this book I have directed the reader's attention to three salient biological principles: (1) the interaction and interdependence of all forms of life from plants to man; (2) the continuous changes that take place in all living things; and (3) the central and underlying role of the habitat. It is the third of these principles that the tragic story of the Sahel illustrates. All living things depend on the habitat in which they live. The desert supports few people, and yet it is people themselves who are largely responsible for the continual growth of Africa's desert areas. The importance of this conclusion—a valid one, even though it has been hotly debated—is that the process can be reversed. It cannot be reversed, as we shall see, by imposing on arid lands the agricultural systems that evolved in Europe or North America, and that are quite unsuited to desert places, where water, not sunshine, is the limiting factor. But sensible land-use activities based firmly on sound ecological principles can reclaim once-fertile areas from their present aridity.

On a large rock in the desert near El Greribat on the borders of Southern Libya and North Chad there is a carved representation of two giraffes. One looks forward and down in the inquisitive way so typical of giraffes when a strange object or movement catches their attention. The second, smaller and apparently younger, is staring at the same object and seems to be seeking the protection of the older animal.

This Ethiopian boy, with his primitive plow drawn by oxen, is working land typical of much of his country. The devastating droughts of the mid-1970s in the mainly agricultural and pastoral economy affected the country's entire political system.

The carving is prehistoric. When you turn away from this boulder, you face the shimmering reflection of the sun from the flat sands of the Sahara. You see no vegetation other than an occasional tuft of dry grass and one or two stunted remnants of a bush, which, for a fleeting moment in the year, might take on some color, but will swiftly shrink back into the twisted agony of the desert's fierce midday heat and midnight icy coldness.

Large animals, you feel sure, could never have lived in this place, and particularly not the giraffe, whose evolution taught it to raise its head high into the branches of trees to gather food. Yet many other ancient carvings of such animals as long-horned cattle and elephants can be found on rocks in the Sahara. Are these just the doodlings of travelers, or do they tell us that the Sahara was once fertile? The giraffes at El Greribat are not just lifeless pictures; they are alive and tense in a way that suggests the artist was living among them, and watching them quite often. From the frequency of such carvings, from remains found in the Sahara, and from evidence of the great Roman rock cisterns in the center of the Negev, we can have little doubt that this desert land was once extremely fertile, and that only in the course of time has it become bleak and arid.

What happened gradually in the past is happening rapidly today: every year an estimated 150 million tons of topsoil are being blown away from Africa south of the Sahara. Starting as a sand spout, or "dust devil," the topsoil climbs high into the sky in a haze that colors the evening sun and the horizon. Caught in high-altitude winds, it is sometimes blown as far as Barbados in the West Indies. Kampala is the principal city of Uganda, in central Africa, where, far away from the desert, there are many lakes and a plentiful supply of rain. Early in 1975, the people of Kampala saw a dust haze over their city for the first time in known history. It was just one more piece of evidence of an onrushing threat to millions of people.

Admittedly, there are reputable scientists who believe that the African deserts are not man-made dust bowls but can be ascribed mainly to the continent's geographical position, almost entirely within 30° of the equator—a zone

Carved on rocks in the Tassili Plateau region of Algeria are very ancient representations of such animals as long-horned cattle and giraffes—large mammals that could not survive today in this or any other part of the Sahara Desert where soil-eroding sand spouts, also known as "dust devils" (right), are much more in evidence than are nourishing blades of grass or leafy branches for such animals to graze or browse upon. Most scientists believe that these and similar carvings in other sections of the expanding Sahara probably indicate that the land was once fertile and that man's irresponsible overuse of it has helped create the arid desert.

marked by dry descending air and low rainfall. Most authorities disagree, however. After all, the region around the Amazon River in South America is even closer to the equator than the basin of the Nile, and yet it is extremely fertile. When we think of the man-made dust bowls of North America, we can easily understand how centuries of deforestation, overgrazing, and erosion are largely responsible for the Sahara. Of course, there must be *some* uncertainty, because we were not there 1000 years ago to watch it happening, but there is no doubt that changes are occurring in our own time that can only be described as the making of deserts by man. Those of us who have lived and worked in Africa have all witnessed the brittle, arid ecology collapsing into degeneracy in the wake of agriculture and grazing cattle; when the land will no longer support cattle, the goats are brought in and they eat everything down to the last stunted thorn tree. By contrast we have also seen how the creation of great waterways held by the dams at Kariba in Zambia and Volta in Ghana have brought irrigation, fish, and green growth to formerly dry places. So we have seen

both sides of the coin, and we know that man has had, and is still having, for better or for worse, a profound influence on the ecology.

We can also go back through history for evidence. In 2000 B.C., King Amenembet I of Egypt boasted: "I grew corn. I loved Heper the Grain God. In every valley the Nile greeted me. None hungered nor thirsted in my reign." In the third century B.C., Hannibal certainly did not get his elephants from central Africa but from somewhere in the north, probably the Atlas Mountains. This means that the habitat must have been suitable for elephants—in other words, rich woodland—which it certainly is not now. More recently, we can read accounts written by such 18th- and 19th-century explorers of the Nile as America's George English, France's Frédéric Cailliaud, and Britain's James Bruce. Cailliaud, a meticulous observer, set out in 1820 on a journey up the Nile to record warfare, massacre, antiquities, and nature. Around the Blue Nile between Halfaya and Sennar (now in the arid Sudan), he saw many ostriches, hippopotamuses, and giraffes, as well as fresh elephant tracks; but at Sennar itself, where, only 50 years earlier,

is happening to the natural world is limited by his very human concept of the difference between a long and short time. Why worry about the future of whales, when there are still a few thousands left—plenty for "a long time to come?" The African desert grows only one or two miles a year—hardly enough to matter. It is the long-term trend (from the human standpoint), however, that tells the all-important story. When, 40 years ago, the blue-whale catch fell from an annual 30,000 to 20,000, conservation action should have been taken ("But there are plenty left!"). When the blue-whale catch fell to 10,000, the species was surely in danger ("But 10,000 is a lot!"). When it fell to 5000 ("Well, 5000 is a good number"), it was almost too late. And now?

And so we tend to be tricked by time scales, by numbers, by greed. What we think, without quite saying it, is: "I'll change my ways if you can prove it'll happen in my lifetime." How wrong that attitude is! The proof that an animal will become extinct or that the Amazon basin will become as arid as the Nile basin can come only when it has happened, and then it is too late.

The Sahara Desert was once fertile. That something could be done to restore at least some

of the fertility is a certainty and a challenge. Before we see the need we must break through the numbers game, and the tricks of biological time scales; this can be achieved by examining the Sahel catastrophe, which, after several years of relentless drought, has brought disaster to millions of people in the sub-Saharan region to the west of northern Africa. Some 22 million people inhabit this area, and US Public Health experts estimate that by late 1972 a minimum of 100,000 deaths had resulted from five years of drought. There have been reports of millions dead and dying, but such exaggerations can actually do a disservice to those they are supposed to be helping. The real disaster is not death; it is the increasing erosion of lands, people, plants, and animals, which results in the displacement of whole populations.

Rehabilitation of the semiarid land that lies south of the Sahara presents a challenge to ecologists. Where there is water, as in the Libyan Kufra Desert (left), grasses and crops can be grown. But attempts to stem desert advance by "dune fixation" (below) can be at best only temporary. An ecological approach to the problem would be to use plants and animals already adapted to this semiarid zone to build self-regulating barriers capable of extending their own boundaries.

Cattle with hardly enough flesh to stretch over their ribs and children whose bellies are swollen from hunger—these are pathetically common sights in the Sahel region of northwestern Africa. The cattle here were photographed in Senegal on the west coast, the children 1500 miles away in Niger; in between and far to the north, east, and south lie still more overgrazed lands inhabited by still more such unfortunates. Only a new policy of internationally sponsored conservation can keep the horror from spreading.

international observers saw in the gathering dust of the Sahel not a cataclysmic situation but an extension or magnification of long-term trends; and they therefore saw no emergency such as would require the necessary drastic measures. Preventive steps would have meant slaughtering cattle, turning them into canned meat and leather. The people would have had to be moved out of desert fringes in advance of their total collapse. Although such actions would have been highly unpopular, they might have saved some of the sick land from the permanent effects of overgrazing and desert formation. But the actions were not taken. In short, the Sahel was being allowed to die. In 1971–2 the Sahara captured not one and a half miles of new territory from the Sahel, but 20 miles.

And what of the future? The international community has plans for a massive aid program to bring water to the surface by sinking more bore holes, and thus to help reestablish a cattle monoculture—the very policy that has already been associated with failure. What guarantee is there of water recharge? What will stop the cattle population from again expanding, denuding the land of vegetation, lowering the water table,

and desiccating surrounding areas. What is to stop it from happening all over again? Based on the present *minimum* rate of desert expansion, by the end of the century another 100,000 square miles of the Sahel will have become desert. Where will the people and their livestock go?

It is clear that land-use policies in Africa and other semiarid regions have failed, and for one reason above all others. Imported from countries where water is abundant, land-use policies have been applied where water is the limiting factor. European and American agriculture evolved in the context of much rain and little sun. In Africa there is much sunshine and little rain. The conditions are different, and therefore different methods should be applied to working the land. This must be obvious, and yet the international community goes on spending its money on centers for cattle-use and on bore holes. The 1974 manifesto of the newly organized International Livestock Center for Africa speaks of fattening animals and of grazing systems. Nowhere does it mention the need for conserving deeprooted vegetation or the browsing basis of the semiarid ecology. Even the FAO report on the program for the rehabilitation of the Sahel area omits

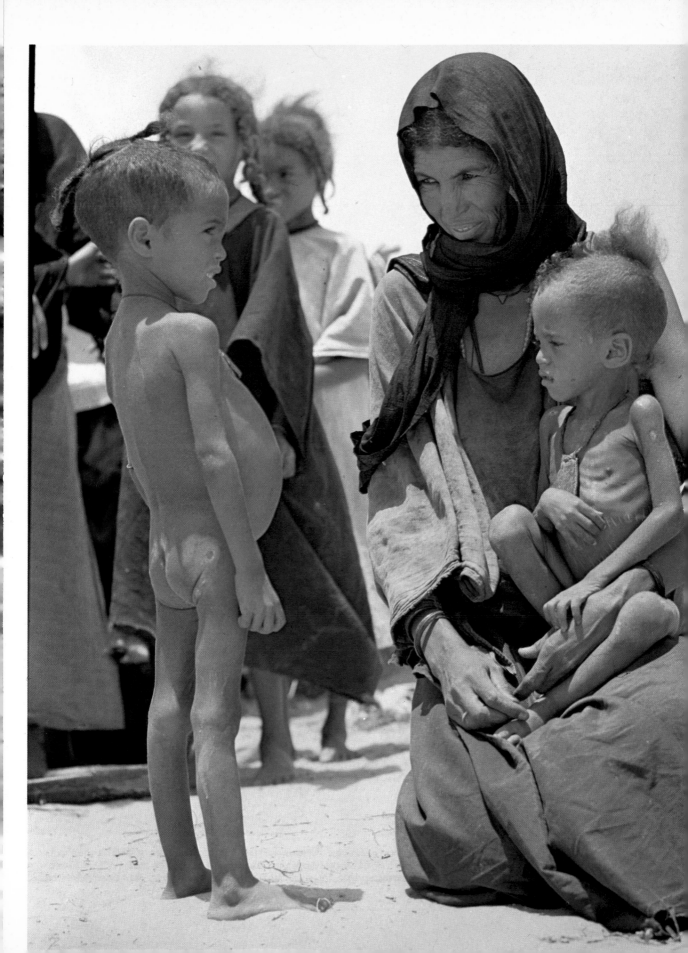

During Ethiopia's terrible drought of 1973, many tankers such as this one brought precious water to remote villages, and grain is still being distributed to the nomads and pastoralists—not only, as here, in the dusty Sahel area of Niger, but throughout the Sahel belt. But aid from the outside world does not actually help to solve the basic problem: land mismanagement.

encroachment, and hardship and famine to large numbers of people. If the pessimists are wrong, however, and desert encroachment is the result of mismanagement, then correct management should lead to a reversal of the process. In any case, something has to be done if the past history of overgrazing, drought, and famine is not to be repeated. You have to either move the people back from the advancing desert or solve the

problem of arresting the spread of the desert. The current approach to Sahel favors the latter view, and in 1974 the Food and Agriculture Organization of the United Nations published a report on a program for the "rehabilitation" of the Sahel region that reflects present expert thinking on the matter.

The FAO document is concerned, amongst other things, with the development of drought-

resistant crops. But this really does not contribute to the solution of the desert encroachment problem; it only offers a solution as to *how to live with it*. In which case the situation could be made worse by encouraging people to live closer to the fringes and expose themselves to the risk of severe drought.

A proposal that sounds effective is the establishment of a green barrier of gum, or acacia trees. There are disadvantages, however. First, a green belt of one species of tree is an agricultural solution—in effect a monoculture. Monocultures are not natural, and require intensive management; the money, energy, and manpower required to maintain the belt will be high. Secondly, because the monoculture is unnatural it does not provide for pollinating insects or seed-dispersal agents such as birds or animals. Hence, because the monoculture cannot extend its own boundaries, someone else has to do it, again adding to the high cost of management and development. It might be that some of the cost could be recovered in timber, but that will only be after many years. Thirdly, many countries are involved in the Sahel and many wild animals still live in this region.

Either the wildlife will have to be exterminated or the whole barrier belt must be fenced off to protect the sapling trees.

The principles of ecology and conservation offer a different approach, one which in my view is better but which is not considered in the FAO document: the use of the semiarid ecosystem as a tool for rehabilitation. This amounts to developing and encouraging the diverse plants and animal species adapted to semiarid conditions to make use of their interdependence. Thus the diversity of plants encourages pollinating insects and birds that in turn maintain and encourage the diversity of plants. The tall deeprooted trees provide shade and moisture for the smaller plants and also provide food and water for the semiarid-adapted animals. The animals can then be used to manage the vegetation. The giraffe would thin the undersurface of the tall, candelabra acacias, eland and kudu trim the bushes, and oryx and addax would operate on open grassy regions. But the animals themselves require control to prevent disease and overbrowsing and that in turn means animal husbandry—and, ultimately, food for the people.

Another obvious property of animals in such a role—but one which is seldom recognized—is

One way to use a semiarid ecosystem without misusing it would be to domesticate wild native animals that are adapted to drought conditions instead of relying on conventional livestock, which can thrive only when water is plentiful. During the drought of 1975, the Galla tribesmen of Ethiopia (left) could find so little water for their livestock that they had to ration it severely. The little leather bowls from which thirsty cattle were forced to drink could hardly have held enough to assuage the thirst of a tiny dog. Africa's indigenous elands, on the other hand, can live comfortably for up to 18 months without direct access to water. Adequately fed and sleek on the Tanzanian farm pictured below, they are well worth the care given them, for their meat is tender and delicious, and their milk contains twice as much nourishing protein and fat as the milk from conventional domestic cows. Moreover, the eland does not succumb to many of the diseases that bedevil nonindigenous farmland beasts.

that each animal is a water trap. Each large herbivore is about 70 per cent water. The deep-rooted plants bring up water from the deep water tables; during the heat of the day the leaves evaporate water, maintaining the humidity for the smaller plants. The water content of the leaves falls as water is lost to the environment. The rate of loss is controlled by the leaves, but may reach a level at which evaporation is stopped. During the heat of the day the animals sleep in the shade. As the cool of the evening approaches the leaves replenish their water supplies and it is during the night that animals literally drink from the deep water tables by eating the leaves. This technique combined with their physiological and anatomical adaptations means that the animals can dispense with surface water, satisfying all their water requirements from the food they eat. In this way both the semiarid-adapted plants and the animals help to trap water within the environment. Even at the end of the dry season deeprooted acacias and balanites can be seen still carrying green leaves whilst everything else is dry. The proof of the efficacy of this ecosystem is simply that it evolved over a period of many millions of years to meet the rigors of the semiarid tropics.

So we can see that the development of the semiarid ecosystem as a tool for subdesert rehabilitation has a number of advantages. First, it is capable of a high degree of self-management. Secondly, with encouragement it is self-regenerating and can extend its own boundaries through its built-in seed dispersal agents. Thirdly, it provides food as well as timber. The 2600-mile stretch of the Sahel is so big that any solution to desert encroachment on this scale must possess these properties. The ecological approach has all these useful properties, whereas the monoculture solution does not.

Applying the principles of ecology and conservation to the rehabilitation of the Sahel prompts the further questions: What is the appropriate method of land-use in the developing world? Should the adaptations of indigenous animals adapted to semiarid conditions be used to develop a new system of animal husbandry for food in regions where conventional agriculture and cattle are not suited?

In 1974 the International Aid Donors established the International Livestock Center for Africa (ILCA), whose manifesto I have already mentioned: they did not question the efforts of the projected ILCA program on the ecology of Africa. That program, as set forth in the manifesto, ignores the potential of Africa's indigenous resources—resources that evolved biologically as adaptations to the special conditions of Africa—despite the recognized fact (which is even recognized in reports by the FAO) that the greatest limitations to extending animal production in Africa are climate and disease to which indigenous animals are adapted but nonnative animals are not. Why did the ILCA not consider the obvious course of encouraging and supporting the development of native African animals and their ecosystem?

Cows are not indigenous to Africa. Probably the early European colonizers did not realize this. They saw Africans with large herds of cattle and took it for granted that they were part of the scenery. The facts that the cattle were barely flesh and bones with little meat—no African would try to sell or barter a cow at midday because the overhead sun accentuated the shadows from its protruding ribs—and that these scrawny cattle were surrounded by fat wild animals many times their size did not penetrate most minds. An occasional voice spoke out in favor of domesticating certain wild African species, but tradition was too strong. So what did the highly influential European settlers, colonizers, and traditionalists do? They encouraged the extension of relatively nonproductive cattle-grazing, and slaughtered millions of useful animals that were splendidly adapted to the heat, stress, and water limitations of the African climate. During the first half of this century, the bubal hartebeest, rufous gazelle, mountain zebra, giant eland, sable antelope, and scimitar-horned oryx either became extinct or are on the brink and listed in the *Red Data Book* of threatened species. In most of Africa the extermination process has been so successful that the remaining wild animals are found only within the boundaries of national parks. If the European settlers and administrators of African colonies had listened to the biologists and conserved Africa's indigenous resources for the sake of their usefulness, the continent could have doubled the world supply of edible meat by now.

Instead, the importation of cattle also brought the scourge of rinderpest to Africa's wildlife as well as to her domestic herds—an epidemic that started in Ethiopia and traveled all the way down to the Cape. Rinderpest was new to game animals, hordes of which were destroyed along with the livestock. The significance of this epidemic, which raged at the turn of the century (and has been a problem virtually ever since), has never been fully documented, but it robbed millions of people of high-quality animal foods and was probably an important factor in turning the nutritional tables in Africa. The sudden loss of great quantities of wild and domestic animals meant that people had to survive somehow on poor-quality staple foods; in this sense, cattle and rinderpest can be seen as a primary cause of today's widespread malnutrition. Many areas, such as Bulemezi and the Kafu, never recovered and remain empty. Ever since 1900 a return of rinderpest has lurked in the background as a constant threat to wild and domestic herds, although we can now control it with a vaccine.

As for indigenous African diseases—fly-borne diseases, for instance, such as trypanosomiasis—

Although the warthog may not be beautiful, hunters look upon its meat as a delicacy. Yet most Africans reject it. It seems odd that many edible wild animals are aimlessly destroyed, while expensive, sickly cattle continue to be pampered.

the continent's native animals are adapted to tolerate *them*, but cows are not. Traditionalism has therefore decreed that the wild animals that do not mind being bitten by tsetse flies must be exterminated in order to make room for the kind of animals that succumb! And that is not the most curious part of the story. The tsetse often lives on small animals that cannot be shot from the convenience of a motor vehicle, and so there is only one sure way to eliminate the trypanosome-carrying fly entirely: because the fly can breed only in an environment of shade and moisture, you must get rid of the trees that provide such amenities. Between 1961 and 1965, millions of dollars were spent on clearing the trees and bushes in a number of areas, while the animals were shot and the carcasses left to rot in the sunshine. There was too much meat for the transport. In one year in one small area the size of an English county, some 2000 tons of meat fed vultures, hyenas, and ants. That was enough to provide two pounds of meat a week for every man, woman, and child in half a dozen African townships for a year. Then came a surprise: the gentle grasses and herbs that had lived in the shade of the trees and provided food for domestic and wild animals could not take the full exposure to the sun; they died off and were replaced by hard, inedible lemon grass.

The tsetse fly is only one of many problems for foreign animals. The ticks in some areas also carry a fatal disease with which the indigenous animals had learned to live. African swine fever attacked pigs that colonizers imported into the continent at considerable expense. The mortality rate among these nonindigenous animals exposed to swine fever was of the order of 98 per cent. Imported pigs caught this lethal disease from indigenous wild pigs, to which the fever was hardly more troublesome than a cold in the nose. So the European traditionalists had to erect strong fences to keep these strange-looking warthogs and bush-pigs out, and did their best to kill all wild pigs in the area.

In a world in which high-quality food is becoming a hard currency, it is odd that meat from

Cracking, sun-baked mud is a poor habitat even for lizards. This one has died because, like countless other wild animals, it could not survive after all vegetation had disappeared through climatic changes and mismanagement of the soil.

the wild bovids, the antelopes, and the warthog, looked upon as delicacies by experienced hunters, are generally rejected. In fact, the flesh of the warthog is delicious; it tastes rather like a cross between turkey and pork. The flavor of eland is not too unlike that of beef, except that eland lacks the high grease content of stall-fed cattle and is more like veal. An adult eland can weigh between 1500 and 2000 pounds, and its meat is still tender even if the animal is killed at more than 10 years of age. For 25 million years, these and other African animals have evolved physiological and behavioral mechanisms to defend themselves against heat, drought, and endemic disease. The oryx, for example, has a water requirement only one fifth that of cattle, and its meat is excellent. Why, then, try to destroy such food sources for the sake of less adaptable—and thus far less dependable—ones?

In the mid-1960s, Dr. Richard Taylor, an American scientist working with the East African Veterinary Research Organization, became interested in the physiology of African herbivores. How was it, he wondered, that the eland and oryx were capable of lasting through 18-month-long periods of drought without access to surface water—a feat that many naturalists,

No other substance in the desert is more desirable—or harder to find—than water. This well at Iférouane in Niger is a focal point whose importance to man and beast cannot be overstated. Wells sometimes run dry, however, with consequent death to cattle, whereas edible native animals require only a fraction of the water needed by the traditionally preferred livestock.

Conservation in Action

If man is the enemy of nature, why and how should he try to conserve the natural world? An answer must begin with the realization that, paradoxically, the conservation idea is part of man's own nature. Taboos, self-denying ordinances, rationing laws, the killing of males only at certain times of the year—such things are actually conservation measures that emerged from Stone Age man's confrontation with the effects of the Pleistocene overkill. The rules became more complex as people became more proficient at using tools. Hunting areas became the prerogative of certain communities, and wars were fought over the possession of water, food, and mineral riches. To conserve their animals, the kings of ancient Persia enclosed hunting areas and called them "paradises." The Norman kings of England introduced forest laws to protect the supply of game animals. The Vikings established a seabird-hunting culture in the Hebrides, in the Faeroes, and in Iceland, with regulations as to cropping season and the size of the cull. Such practices are forerunners of modern hunting and fishing laws and the creation of national parks and reserves.

There has always been a conflict, however, between our desire to conserve useful species and our greed—a battle between the "good" side of us, which wants to protect living things not only for their usefulness but for their beauty, and the "bad" side, which kills ruthlessly, either to exploit a free resource or under the name of sport. The good and bad are not as easily defined as some people think. For instance, the person who hunts is not necessarily anticonservation. There are plenty, to be sure, who kill animals for the sheer pleasure of it. I recall one rich tourist in Africa who shot 11 buffaloes "just for fun" on a single day's shooting, and boasted about it. Such blood-thirstiness is indeed degrading. But the impulse to kill is part of man's biological makeup and must be understood as such. In order to

This—a common sight during the Minnesota hunting season— is not necessarily a picture of thoughtless cruelty. The young man who kills a bull moose for sport is obeying natural human instinct, and he and his companions may well be ardent conservationists, for there can be no hunting without wildlife.

survive, humanity has always had to do things that may seem very unpleasant to some. Man evolved as a hunter-gatherer: during this time, killing was part of his business.

Well-intentioned people who criticize the hunting fraternity for killing a deer for the larder may be forgetting that it could have been killed rather nastily by some other predator if the human hunter had not got there first. If there were no predators, the deer might well have succumbed to slow starvation in winter when overpopulation of its species exceeded the food supply. Perhaps it would be nice if we could stop wearing leather shoes and eating meat, but such things, which we can have only as a result of killing animals, have been a necessity for many societies. It seems likely that we should be doing something biologically unnatural if we all became herbivores. Advocates of absolute vegetarianism may be right when they argue that five times as much protein can be obtained from the vegetables grown on an acre of land as we get from animals supported

by the same area. Protein is certainly important for body growth, but recent research suggests that organic compounds called *lipids* are important for the growth of the brain—the outstanding biological development in the human species. And meat apparently contains considerably more of the essential lipids than do plants.

This interesting finding seems to support the theory that human beings thrive best on a mixture of foods. To drastically change our traditional and evolution-tested diet might be a risky denial of our biological heritage. That is why such shortcuts to nourishment as bypassing animal food and eating only vegetables are seldom advocated by biologists. The upward thrust of man's evolutionary history tells us he has been associated with both plant and animal foods, and indeed meat may have predominated. The only completely herbivorous ape is the gorilla, which, like the cow, has a large body but a relatively small brain. This, too, would suggest that eating flesh—i.e. killing—is part of man's biology.

Stalking deer in Scotland. Because these amateur huntsmen have a personal stake in keeping the moors plentifully stocked, they are more likely than not to be extremely generous contributors to well-organized conservation programs.

Strange as it may seem, a major contribution to conservation has been made by the world's hunters. Take the situation in America as an example. After more than a century of pillage, during which bison fell to the firearm and forests were cleared by the saw, the Americans did an about-face, and they have led the world in restoration work. At the beginning of this century, mule deer, white-tailed deer, elks, pronghorn antelopes, beavers, bears, and wild turkeys survived in North America only in small pockets. Now there are 6 million mule deer, 7 million white-tailed deer, 350,000 elks, and 400,000 pronghorn antelopes in the United States and Canada; beavers and bears have made a significant comeback; and wild turkeys can be found in reason-

able numbers in 40 states. Even the buffaloes now number about 25,000 in the USA alone. And this return has been largely brought about by those who themselves have hunted the animals.

The hunter comes into very close contact with his prey. If he is to be successful, he must know its habits, the type of food it eats, its need of water and shade, and the kind of terrain it prefers. He must also appreciate the special outstanding features or characteristics of the species, so that he can go after an animal with a good head or a fine skin. He has to follow the animal through the bush, and so he must be able to identify its tracks and must be aware of its response to danger. When he finally gets a shot at it, he must know a good deal about its anatomy if he wants to make a clean kill. For all these reasons, the sportsman builds up a relationship with the animals he hunts, and that is why intelligent hunters tend to be ardent conservationists and to plow more money than most non-hunters into conservation programs. Audubon

himself, a renowned bird lover, was also quite a good huntsman.

There are probably more than 18 million hunters in the USA, and they spend over $1000 million annually on their sport. Since 1937 they have also provided major financial support for the Federal Government's wildlife-conservation agency, the Bureau of Sport, Fisheries, and Wildlife, which manages an animal-refuge system covering a total of 32 million acres. In addition, the bureau improves habitats, conducts research, stimulates education (more than 40 US colleges and universities offer wildlife-management courses), and offers free advice to landowners. American hunters harvest well over 2 million large game animals annually; and, apart from trophies and skins, they get more than 225,000 tons of meat from their prey (not including the many millions of birds taken annually). Such figures apply only to legal, permissible killings and therefore indicate the vastness of the wildlife population. There are

This is the kind of vegetarian diet advocated by many warm-hearted animal lovers. Informed conservationists, however, far from opposing the killing of animals for food, recognize the importance of nutrients gained from eating meat.

now probably more large animals in the United States than in Africa—an undeniable achievement for a country that was stamping out its wild creatures less than a century ago.

Hunters, of course, are mainly concerned with games species, whereas the strict conservationist cares about the whole spectrum of wildlife. Still, it is a significant fact that the very delight that man takes in hunting and killing his prey contributes mightily to conservation, because the hunter wants to be sure that there is always plenty of prey for him to stalk. And it is only a small step from hunting reserves to national parks, where animals are also shot, but as a direct conservation measure, to keep animal communities from becoming overpopulated.

North America has set the pace in creating national parks where all plant and animal life is protected. Of the world's 1400-odd national parks and reserves, Russia has 80, Great Britain and Australia each have 70-odd, France has only 17, and the United States and Canada together have around 340. The two North American countries, of course, can more easily turn great tracts of land over to nature than can the thickly populated countries of western Europe. Thus, Yellowstone in the United States covers an area of well over 2 million acres, and the US has 15 other parks of over 250,000 acres each. Canada, a land of very wide open spaces, does even better; 17 of her national parks cover areas of 250,000 acres or more, and one of them— Wood Buffalo in northeastern Alberta—is approximately 11 million acres.

The great national parks of all the continents, including those of Africa, have taught us a three-fold lesson. First, every large-scale conservation area has a limited capacity for human tourists; beyond a certain point, deterioration in tourist enjoyment and in the park's flora and fauna occurs. Secondly, no national park can succeed at conserving wildlife and scenery without some form of management. Lastly, there are places where the national-park concept is not appropriate, because other needs have priority. This last cautionary lesson is particularly applicable to parks in developing countries. The countries of Africa tend to justify the creation of wildlife reserves on the ground that they bring in the tourists. But there are those who argue that it might be better economics to use the land for the people of the country by turning it over to agriculture. That seems a short-sighted point of view to the conservationist, but it is hard to convince hungry people that they should conserve their resources for future generations.

When a wildlife conservation and management bill was presented to the Kenya Parliament in 1975, it had to be withdrawn because of strong objections on the ground that it sought to protect wildlife more than human beings. Setting aside land for conservation, said many Kenyans, conflicted with the country's immediate needs. Their basic argument, flavored with some of the

bitterness left over from the days of European colonialism, is a strong one, not at all easy to refute: "The Europeans have achieved agricultural success by destroying their own wildlife; we need that same kind of success and are not going to forgo it just to conserve African wildlife for the Europeans." That attitude is far removed from the high ideals of United Nations efforts to encourage conservation through national parks,

The bears in America's Yellowstone National Park are among the park's best-known, best-loved features. But even national-park animals must sometimes be killed in order to save wildlife communities from the bad effects of overpopulation.

but it is understandable. If confronted with an appeal by the people to use the Lamai Wedge in the Serengeti for grazing domestic livestock and a counterappeal by the World Wildlife Fund not to let them, the Tanzanian authorities will inevitably listen more attentively to the needs of the people, and who is to blame them?

National parks are a fine thing, but in the long run they are a luxury that not every nation can manage. It is easy for a rich country such as the United States to increase its agriculturally non-productive conservation lands, because it can afford to be more concerned with conserving certain environments than with making money or food out of them. In the developing nations the situation is very different. And that is why conservation through utilization seems such an attractive alternative. If the survival of wild

plants and animals is threatened because people need to put economically useful things in their place, a sensible way to ensure their survival is to use *them*. In order to make use of them, of course, we must find ways of protecting them, so that they remain a continuing resource. Let us look now at some object lessons in conservation through utilization.

Red deer were introduced into New Zealand for the weekend sport of early settlers, and they flourished there so heartily that they began to do serious damage to the trees that clothe the island's hillsides and hold down the soil. By the 1950s so much soil was being eroded and washed down from the hills that it was threatening the course of valley rivers. Worried farmers insisted that the deer must be eliminated, and so the animals were categorized as vermin, and an official plan to destroy them was set in motion in the early 1960s. Then came the realization that they were shooting venison, so why not sell it? In the first year the deer meat brought in $50,000; in the second $600,000; in the third $2½ million; in the fourth $5 million. Ready markets were found in Europe (mainly West Germany) and the United States. Very soon, of course, the deer were taken off the list of vermin, and controlled utilization was put into practice. Today they are no longer permitted to denude the hillsides; but, far from being eliminated, they are regarded as an economic asset.

The saiga antelope lives in Kazakhstan in the USSR. It spends part of the time in the mountains and part on the flat plains, across which sandstorms sweep ferociously. Neither man nor his domestic animals can tolerate these sandstorms, which can choke animals to death; but the saiga has evolved unusual nostrils with downward-facing flaps, and it can virtually close these in a storm and filter sand-free air into its lungs. The local people, unable to keep large numbers of livestock, had been shooting the saiga for meat for so many years that they had reduced the saiga population to about 300 by the 1930s. At this point it became clear that without a moratorium on shooting, this remarkable creature would be lost forever, and so no further killing was permitted. Now the saiga population has recovered, but unauthorized shooting is still forbidden. Instead, managed culling yields more than 6000 tons of meat a year to the Russian economy, in addition to leather and other animal products.

In South Africa some 5000 farmers maintain a variety of wildlife on their farms, sharing an estimated population of 250,000 springbok and 85,000 blesbok. Veterinary restrictions limit the outlet of meat from such animals but techniques of mass capture have already been worked out and the South African Government has now put forward an impressive environmental program, part of which will eventually involve the rational utilization of wildlife.

The capybara, living in flooded grasslands in Venezuela, again occupies an ecological niche unsuitable to domestic stock. At present Venezuela sells nearly 400 tons of capybara meat

Native animals are often more suitable than imported ones for other purposes than food. The African zebra, for example, can be ridden like a horse, and it is much less susceptible than horses to the dangerous disease of trypanosomiasis.

This lodge in Kenya's Tsavo National Park is the starting place for many an exciting safari. Most of Africa's developing countries feel that they can afford national parks only when, as here, these can be maintained as a profitable tourist attraction.

Intelligent management can make an economic virtue of an ecological necessity. Red deer such as this were once categorized as vermin in New Zealand; now they are protected and controlled, and their meat earns millions of New Zealand dollars.

The saiga antelope of southeastern Russia (right) was nearly exterminated by meat-hungry hunters before the government intervened in the 1930s. Controlled utilization since then has meant new life for the species—and over 6000 tons of meat a year, too.

annually, but makes no use of their skins. In other South American countries their pelts are used as leather and fetch high prices.

The water buffalo of Australia is not indigenous to that country, but was introduced in the 1820s. There was a spasmodic trade in their hides, but by 1959 it had become uneconomic to shoot them for hides alone and a small meat industry was started. The products sold mainly to the pet food industry at low prices, but some was certified and sold for human consumption. Don Tulloch of the Animal Industry and Agricultural Branch in the Northern Territories comments that it is desirable to domesticate these animals fully because by 1971 the certified buffalo-meat industry alone earned about A $1¼ million, the price accelerating as people overcame their initial prejudice to the meat.

I could describe many similar developments, but the moral is already abundantly clear: intelligent management can make an economic virtue of an ecological necessity. In some cases, wild animals can perform other services for the economy, apart from providing food and skins. Take the manatee as an example. Manatees are herbivorous mammals that live in warm water, whether fresh or salt. Like their near relative, the dugong, they graze on underwater grasses that few other animals will eat. They have such an excellent appetite for waterweeds that they have been used in Guyana as weed clearers. In fact, Dr. Ricardo Bertram, a marine biologist at Cambridge University, has suggested that they could well be used for keeping tropical reservoirs and hydroelectric dams free from weeds as a sideline to producing meat (which, incidentally, is of very good quality). Unfortunately they are very easily killed, and the prospect for their survival in numbers large enough to become truly useful to man is bleak unless some form of slaughter control is soon adopted.

Naturally, there are problems connected with any program for wildlife utilization. For instance, if you want to use a uniquely adapted animal source for food, you must make sure that your animals are free from disease, both of the kind that will undermine their own health and of the kind that might be transmitted to man. Disease control is essential, and this means that the animals must be handled, which in turn means that they must be tamed, which in turn necessitates domestication in some form or other. Some conservationists are opposed to domestication because it is likely to change and distort the species. That need not happen, however, if the true value of a species is utilized—that is, if the animals are kept in an extensive free-range situation in which their specialized adaptations to climatic zones, plants, and terrain are taken into consideration.

The outstanding success of buffalo domestication in the Indian state of Gujarat is worth mentioning. Many Indians depend on milk to improve the quality of their meager diet, and not long ago a project called "Operation Flood" was launched

in the Kaira District of Gujarat. Buffaloes were domesticated for the sake of their milk alone, and "Operation Flood" set out to produce a flood of milk in rural areas, which it succeeded in doing. Milk is now produced in over 700 villages, each with its own cooperative that buys, tests, and bulks the milk. This is not intended to be an exercise in conservation, but it *is* that, and much more. The buffaloes are being conserved, the people are being conserved, and the quality of life is being improved.

As Dr. V. Kurien, who directs the "Flood" project, puts it: "When they see that their veterinary doctor can cure their animals of diseases previously fatal . . . when they learn to feed a cow in the last three months of pregnancy even though she is dry, when they see disinfectant being used to keep flies down at the milk-collection center . . . then do they not . . . experience the meaning of health care?" He adds his hope that the rural people may also be coming to realize that "if it is right to feed a pregnant cow, it is even more desirable to feed a pregnant human mother," and that as they learn about artificial insemination in buffaloes, they may also begin to understand the possibilities of subjecting the human reproductive process to control. So this use of animals integrates conservation, human survival, and those facets of life that can raise the standards of an impoverished part of the Third World. It is conservation at its best.

Conservation through utilization may have drawbacks, but it is at least a realistic approach, recognizing that wildlife and man are in competition and that wildlife will lose out unless man has good reasons for keeping the wild species alive. The inestimable value of the genetic potential of such animals for our use is a most powerful argument for assuring their survival. As I pointed out earlier, even the lowly dung beetle turned out to have an unsuspected significance for agriculture. The potential of oryx, addax, and other semiarid-adapted species, lies in their ability to thrive on only one fifth as much water as cattle do. Reindeer, red deer, and other Northern Hemisphere animals are proving their value to man in their own habitats. And so on. Meanwhile, our scientists are increasingly pointing out that we do not know as much as we thought we did about the interdependence of man and nature. And there is general agreement that as we use up the earth's store of fossilized energy and water reserves, we must inevitably become more reliant on nature.

We used to think we could bend the living earth to our will, but it looks now as though we were wrong. We can indeed use nature, but we must work with rather than against nature. We must begin by understanding her laws and that means the search for knowledge and the dissemination of that knowledge. We need the biological banks of wild reserves if for no other reason than that our present hold on this planet is insecure. Our knowledge of the world tells us that we shall have to work toward a completely new philosophy of land use based on the capacity of the ecosystem for regeneration.

I have dealt with the utilization aspect at some length because it is an unfamiliar and highly

Two examples of wildlife conserved because of—and by means of—utilization: the Australian water buffalo (above), once shot indiscriminately for its hide alone, now supports a thriving buffalo-meat industry; and the capybara of Venezuela (right), which is a large edible rodent, brings in substantial revenues to its native land through the sale to other South American countries of both its meat and its skin. Neither animal is suitable for domestication, and so they are kept under protection in extensive free-range situations.

important subject. A more traditional approach to the theme of conservation in action, however, would be to think of it in terms of the societies that are dedicated to conservation. There are many of these with specialized interests, but I should like to mention three of them in which I am particularly interested: the Royal Society for the Protection of Birds (RSPB), the Fauna Preservation Society (FPS), and the National Audubon Society.

The RSPB is a British organization, started in 1889 as a protest against the trade in feathers for women's hats, which was responsible for the destruction of thousands of egrets, herons, and birds of paradise. Today the society, without having changed its name, directs much of its fire against the commercial use of fur and skins from rare species. But it also continues to carry on its flight for endangered birdlife in and around Britain. Ever since the 1920s, for instance, it has kept a lookout for oil pollution and toxic chemicals. It has purchased sanctuaries, and it has stimulated research, legislation, and education, all aimed toward its one goal of conservation. Recently it published a powerful, well-documented report on the cruel importation of wild birds—canaries, parrots, and many beautiful rare species—into Britain; the report *All Heaven in a Rage* tells of the carnage when birds captured in far-off places die in transit or are unfed and unwatered at airports. Some 600,000 birds are imported into Britain every year, and another half-million pass through in transit to other countries. The world bird trade is probably at least an annual 5 million, and as many as 70 per cent of some consignments perish somewhere on the way. Again, the argument for conservation through utilization proves its validity. You cannot continue trapping wild bird species indefinitely without bringing them to the brink of destruction. Those who want to trade in birds must breed them. Breeding, like domestication of larger animals, will take the pressure off the wild resources.

The Fauna Preservation Society (FPS) is an international body whose objective is the protection of all wild animal species. Nearly 20 years ago, when the Kariba Dam in Rhodesia was made operative, the FPS saved many hundreds of marooned animals from starvation by transporting them out of the region. We even know the precise numbers of the creatures they saved: 35 aardvarks, 168 bushbucks, 21 bushpigs, 309

Buffaloes have been successfully domesticated in the Indian state of Orissa, as well as elsewhere in the subcontinent, for their excellent milk and nourishing meat. Although the objective is not primarily conservation, great numbers of two rather important species are kept healthily alive as the end result of such projects: buffaloes and human beings!

duikers, 33 genets, 469 impalas, 33 mongooses, 12 sable antelopes, 236 steinbucks, 160 warthogs, 73 waterbucks, and so on. The organization is also almost solely responsible for having forestalled the extinction of the Arabian oryx by flying the tiny handful left in the desert halfway across the world, to California and Arizona sanctuaries. And its powerful political lobbies have gradually persuaded several Western governments to pass conservation laws relating to trading in endangered species and their products, importing live animals, and protecting various wild animals and plants.

The National Audubon Society, which has its offices in New York, was founded in 1905 as a kind of living memorial to John Audubon, whose great work of art, *The Birds of America*, has been called "the most magnificent monument yet raised by art to science." Audubon was not only interested in birds; with the naturalist John Bachman he worked on a book about the quadrupeds of America, which was completed in 1854,

three years after his death. So the society that bears his name, like the others I have mentioned, is interested in all forms of wildlife and land-use. Among its stated aims is a determination to support all measures that help to conserve energy, to abate environmental pollution, and to control human birthrates. Such aims may seem to encroach on other fields than that of wildlife conservation. But the interdependence within nature should not be forgotten nor should we forget that the fuel crisis and pollution, as well as the need for conservation, are all aspects of the almost insurmountable problem posed by human overpopulation—conservation is not just about wildlife, it is also about us.

Biology, as I have pointed out, is concerned with change. If we leave everything to nature, nature will change everything, as she has always done in the past and will continue to do if left unchecked. Hence, conservation for the good of the human race can be effective only if we are able to control nature through careful management. Evolution has now reached a point in the history of our planet when we must either take intelligent control or let nature—including our own raw nature—control us.

Yet, regrettably, conservation is new to urban man, let alone agricultural man who runs a continuous battle with wildlife and the elements. Education is the vital tool to put over the conservation message. It is typical of man that he puts university faculties that deal with war before faculties of conservation. Education is the only way urban man can learn about conservation, for in the last analysis it is the sum total of people's effort that counts. Everyone must be involved in conservation and there are a number of ways in which the message can spread: First, education teaches people the basic principles of biology and the need for conservation. Second, involvement of willing people in, say, the clearing of village duck ponds, or other similar voluntary work, wins converts. Third, industry spreads the message when it spontaneously (or through pressure) clears up after itself. For example, gravel pits, which used to be left as stagnant holes are, more and more, being rehabilitated as small lakes and watering places.

A few decades ago, birds were being slain to provide feathers for adornments such as the headdress worn onstage by London glamor girl Jessie Matthews. Today, thanks to bird-protection societies, such cruelty is forbidden in the Western World.

When Rhodesia's Kariba Dam became operative, a large number of animals were drowned or marooned, but hundreds—such as this waterbuck—were saved in a rescue program devised and supported by the international Fauna Preservation Society.

Fourth, planners, too, can impress people enormously when, for example, tunnels are made for badgers when a huge motorway crosses their paths. Fifth, zoological gardens and safari parks can be centers for breeding rare and endangered species. Unfortunately, many zoos and safari parks are concerned more with "exhibition," than with breeding. Such places act as a severe drain on resources. Others are satisfied with one generation of breeding but that is not good enough; they can still fail to reproduce in captivity even after the second generation. One will not be certain that the conditions are correct until at least three generations have been born in captivity. Sixth, pressure groups and conservation societies who lobby governments to introduce conservation laws are especially effective.

The reality of the present situation is that all wildlife is threatened. The evolution of large mammals and even of primates is finished. There are a few hundred gorillas and a few thousand chimpanzees left, but there are 4,000,000,000 people.

The last few thousand years has seen the decline in residual wildlife and the evolution of man. Man is now at a critical point, and his own survival is in doubt. The future is going to require greater self-sufficiency as fresh water and the fossil treasures of energy are used up. Conservation in its broadest sense is the key to self-sufficiency, which is the key to our own survival.

We shall need the genetic information stored in wildlife, we shall need open spaces for recreation and stimulation of ideas. We shall also need the conservation ideal as a new ethic.

In the past, religion was the main source of morality, but morality was expressed in terms of one man to another. Man felt he had a direct divine sanction to exploit nature and her resources. We now know the world's resources are finite and in the long run our own survival depends on using those resources within the limits of their capacity for regeneration.

This is not to say that religious philosophy is inadequate, but the times have changed since we were told to go forth, multiply, and take dominion over all things. Both the religious and humanist philosophers argued the case for justice and morality as it affected man. This stance has now been superseded by events and morality must extend from man to wildlife, the land, and its waters. Why should one stop consideration of the moral code with man? Water, soil, plants, ani-

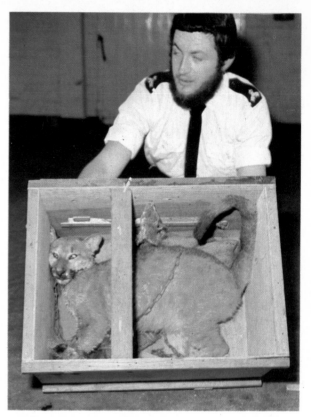

This dead puma exemplifies the carelessness with which many living animals are shipped around the world for exhibition in zoos. The puma was dead when it reached London Airport, partway along on its journey. It was packed in too small a crate with too little ventilation and without the live food pumas need. (What looks like a snake's head is a bit of packaging material.)

mals, and man are intimately woven into a pattern about which we know little.

Felipe Benarides of Peru, whose work in saving the vicuña won him the first Paul Getty Prize for Conservation, said:

"The most advanced nation in the world has sent man to the moon, while the poorer nations are barely able to survive and it is even less likely that the animal kingdom, persecuted by man, will do so for much longer."

The totality of this conservation message is enormous. Yet there is hope. I believe that hope depends on three main factors—first, recognizing the value of wildlife for man's future needs; second, recognizing the need for recreation; third, extending our views on moral philosophy to be not just the relationship between man and man, but between man and the environment on which he has depended for his evolution and will depend for his future.

Very little water left anywhere here—and certainly not a drop to drink! How long can man himself survive if he goes on fouling his rivers, polluting the atmosphere, and using up the earth's treasures? Conservation demands more of us than just an effort to clear away the refuse of the past, as these men are doing. We need to start planning now for the future protection of our entire ecosystem.

137

Wildlife Parks of the World

*Selected by M. J. Ross-Macdonald,
Editor of *The World Wildlife Guide*
(Threshold, London ; Viking, New York)

Not shown on map
Antarctica (open to
tourism since 1968)

BSa	=	Bird Sanctuary	NR	= Nature Reserve
CA	=	Conservation Area	NWR	= National Wildlife Refuge
FR	=	Fauna Reserve	P	= Park
GR	=	Game Reserve	PA	= Protection Area
GSa	=	Game Sanctuary	PP	= Provincial Park
MA	=	Management Area	R	= Refuge
NC	=	Nature Conservation Territory	Res	= Reserve
NM	=	National Monument	Sa	= Sanctuary
NNR	=	National Nature Reserve	SGR	= State Game Reserve
NP	=	National Park	SP	= State Park

* A representative selection from among the world's many thousand parks, reserves, and sanctuaries. All the parks shown here play an important part in conservation and offer the visitor opportunities to observe the wildlife they contain. Political boundaries are drawn only where they are necessary to show the location of parks.

New Zealand
1 Fiordland NP
2 Mt Cook NP
3 Westland NP
4 Arthur's Pass NP
5 Tasman NP
6 Egmont NP
7 Tongariro NP
8 Urewera NP
Fiji
9 Naqaranibuluti NC
10 Ravilevu NR

UNITED STATES OF AMERCIA
Pacific States
11 Hawaii Volcanoes NP (Hi)
12 Haleakala NP (Hi)
13 Aleutian Is NWR (Alaska)
14 Clarence Rhode NWR (Alaska)
15 Mt McKinley NP (Alaska)
16 Kenai National Moose Range (Alaska)
17 Olympic NP (Wash)
18 Mt Rainier NP (Wash)
19 Crater Lake NP (Ore)
20 Klamath NWR (Ore)
21 Sacramento NWR (Calif)
22 Yosemite NP (Calif)
23 Kern-Pixley NWR (Calif)
Mountain States
24 Desert NWR (Nev)
25 Bryce Canyon NP (Utah)
26 Bear River NWR (Utah)
27 National Bison Range (Mont)
28 Glacier NP (Mont)
29 Bowdoin NWR (Mont)
30 Medicine Lake NWR (Mont)
31 Yellowstone NP (Wyo)
32 Grand Teton NP and National
   Elk Refuge (Wyo)
33 Monte Vista NWR (Colo)
The Southwest
34 Saguaro NM (Ariz)
35 Grand Canyon NP (Ariz)
36 Wichita Mts NWR (Okla)
37 Tishomingo NWR (Okla)
38 Aransas NWR (Tex)
39 Laguna Atascosa NWR (Tex')
40 Santa Anna NWR (Tex)
41 Big Bend NP (Tex)
42 Bosque Apache NWR (N Mex)
The Midwest
43 Quivira NWR (Kan)
44 Kirwin NWR (Kan)
45 Fort Niobrara NWR (Nebr)
46 Wind Cave NP (S Dak)
47 Sand Lake NWR (S Dak)
48 Lake Ilo NWR (N Dak)
49 Slade NWR (N Dak)
50 Des Lacs NWR (N Dak)
51 J Clark Salyer NWR (N Dak)
52 Isle Royale NP (Mich)
53 Kirtland's Warbler Management
   Area (Mich)
54 Ottawa NWR (Ohio)
55 Spring Mill SP (Ind)
56 Horicon NWR (Wis)
57 Upper Mississippi NWR (Minn)
58 Mark Twain NWR (Ill)
59 Flint Hills NWR (Kan)
The South
60 Holla Bend NWR (Ark)
61 Reelfoot NWR (Tenn)
62 Gt Smoky Mts NP (Tenn)
63 Shenandoah NP (Va)
64 Chincoteague NWR (Va)
65 Hungry Mother SP (Va)
66 Wheeler NWR (Ala)
67 Eufaula NWR (Ala)
68 Okefenokee NWR (Ga/Fla)
69 Merritt Is NWR (Fla)
70 Loxahatchee NWR (Fla)
71 Everglades NP (Fla)
72 JN "Ding" Darling NWR (Fla)
73 Delta NWR (La)
74 Yazoo NWR (Miss)
75 Sabine NWR (La)
The Northeast
76 Erie NWR (Pa)
77 Iroquois NWR (NY)
78 Missisquoi NWR (Vt)
79 Moose Horn NWR (Me)
80 Morton NWR (NY)
81 Blackwater NWR (Md)

Mexico
96 Cumbres de Monterrey NP
97 El Cogorron NP
98 Nevado de Colima NP
99 Nevado de Toluca NP
100 Ixtacihuatl-Popocatepetl NP
Guatemala
101 Tikal NP
102 El Pino NP

Ecuador
122 Galápagos Islands

Peru
120 Callao guano stacks
121 Nazca Vicuña Reserve

Canada
82 Glacier NP
83 Kootenay NP
84 Banff NP
85 Jasper NP
86 Cypress Hills PP
87 Prince Albert NP
88 Wood Buffalo NP
89 Duck Hills NP
90 Quetico PP
91 Algonquin PP
92 Laurentides PP
93 Gaspesian PP
94 Fundy NP
95 Cape Breton Highlands NP

Venezuela
103 Sierra Nevada de Merida NP
104 Henri Pittier NP
105 El Avila NP
106 Guatopo NP
107 Canaima NP
Guyana
108 Kaieteur Falls NP

Brazil
109 Paulo Afonso NP
110 Sooretama NP
111 Rio Dole Sa
112 Iguassu Falls NP (see also Argentina)
Argentina
113 Finca El Rey NP
114 Iguacu Falls NP (also
   into Paraguay)
115 Lanin NP
116 Nahuel Huapi NP
117 Los Alerces NP
118 Perito Moreno NP
119 Los Glaciares NP

Europe
92 Pallas-Ounastunturin Kansallispuisto (Finland)
93 Sompio NP (Finland)
94 Oulanka NP (Finland)
95 Ulvinsalo NP (Finland)
96 Vesijako NP (Finland)
97 Vaskijärni NP (Finland)
98 Abisko NP (Sweden)
99 Stora Sjöfallet and Sarek NPs (Sweden)
100 Töfsingdalen NP (Sweden)
101 Ångsö NP (Sweden)
102 Jungfrun NP (Sweden)
103 Dalby Söderskog NP (Sweden)
104 Rondane NP (Norway)
105 North Sea Coast reserves (West Germany)
106 Lüneburger Heide NR (West Germany)
107 Pfälzer Bergland NR (West Germany)
108 Bavarian NP (West Germany)
109 Naarder Meer Sa (Netherlands)
110 Swiss NP
111 Vanoise NP (France) and Gran Paradiso NP (Italy)
112 Camàrgue Sa (France)
113 Pyrenese NP (France & Spain)
114 Sept-Îles BSa
115 Sierra Guadarrama (Spain)
116 Coto de Doñana Res (Spain)
117 Sa de Gerêz (Portugal)
118 Tagus and Sado estuaries (Portugal)
119 Bialowieza NP (Poland)
120 Kampinoski Park Narodowy (Poland)
121 Tatra Mts NP (Poland and Czechoslovakia)
122 Neusiedler Lake and Marchegg NRs (Austria)
123 Retezat NP (Romania)
124 Danube Delta reserves (Romania)
125 Plitvice Lakes NP (Yugoslavia)
126 Hutavo Blato BSa (Yugoslavia)
127 Durmitor NP (Yugoslavia)
128 Abruzzi NP (Italy)
129 Olympus NP (Greece)
130 Lake Manyas Bird Paradise (Turkey)

British Isles
134 Orkneys NNRs
135 St Kilda NNR
136 Cairngorms NP
137 Lake District NP
138 Peak District NP
139 Snowdonia NP
140 North Norfolk Coast Res
141 New Forest
142 Dartmoor NP
143 Wexford Sloughs
144 Cape Clear Observatory

Japan
79 Akan NP
80 Nikko NP
81 Fuji-Hakone-Izu NP

Soviet Union
82 Sichote-Alinskij Zapovednik
83 Barguzinskij Zapovednik
84 Altay Res
85 Aksu-Dzabaglinskij Zapovednik
86 Badchyz Res
87 Astrakhan Res
88 Caucasian Res
89 Oka Terrace Res
90 Bialowieza Forest Res
91 Pečoro-Ilyčskij Zapovednik

Israel
131 Hula Lake NR
132 En-gedi NR
133 Elath Gulf NR

Seychelles
221 Mahé, Cousin, Frigate Is

Malaysia
58 King George V NP
Cambodia
59 Angkor Wat NP
Thailand
60 Erewan Waterfall NP
61 Khao Yai NP
Burma
62 Pidaung GR
Bangladesh
63 Sundarbans GSa
64 Chittagong Hills Tract
India
65 Kaziranga GR
66 Manas GR
67 Jaldapara GR
68 Corbett NP
69 Keoladeo-Ghana Sa
70 Kanha NP
71 Gir Forest Res
72 Mudumalai GR
73 Vedanthangal Sa
74 Ranganthittoo Sa
75 Periyar Sa
Sri Lanka
76 Wilpattu NP
77 Gal Oya NP
78 Ruhuna NP

Madagascar
213 Lokobé Sa
214 Cape Masoala Sa
215 Ankarafantsika Sa
216 Betampona Sa
217 Antsingy Sa
218 Andringitra Sa
219 Tsimanampetsotsa Sa
220 Andohahela Sa

Australia
1 Heron Island Sa
2 Lamington NP
3 Tamborine Mt NP
4 New England NP
5 Warrumbungle NP
6 Blue Mts NP
7 Barren Grounds NR
8 Kosciusko NP
9 Pulletop NR
10 Mallacoota Inlet NP
11 Dowd's Morass SGR
12 Tower Hill SGR
13 Flinders Chase Res
14 Coorong FR
15 Hattah Lakes NP
16 Kinchega NP
17 Ayers Rock NP
18 Walpole Nornalup NP
19 Stirling Range NP
20 John Forrest NP
21 Yanchep NP
22 Kalbarri NP
23 Cape Range NP
24 Fogg Dam PA
25 Patonga Sa
26 Woolwonga Sa
27 Katherine Gorge NP
28 Tanami Desert Sa
29 Atherton Tablelands NP
30 Green Is Sa
31 Dunk Is NP
32 Cradle Mt-Lake St Clair NP (Tasmania)
33 Mt Field NP (Tasmania)

Philippines
34 Callao Cave NP
35 Hundred Is NP
36 Biak-na-bato NP
37 Mt Maikiling NP
38 Naujan Lake NP
39 Caramoan NP
40 Mt Bulusan NP
41 Sohoton Natural Bridge NP
42 Kuapnit-Balinsasayao NP
43 Mainit Hot Spring Sa
44 Liguasan Marsh GR

Indonesia
45 S. M. Langkat NP
46 Gunung Leuser NP
47 Berbak NP
48 Sumatera Selatan NP
49 Udjung Kulon-Panaitan NP
50 Way Kambas NP
51 Kotawaringin/Sampit NP
52 Padang Luwai Res
53 Tangkoko-Batuangus NC
54 Penandjung NP
55 Nusa Barung NC
56 Ardjuna — Lalidjiwa Res
57 S. M. Bali NP

North and western Africa
145 Bou Hedma Sa (Tunisia)
146 Tazekka NP (Morocco)
147 Toubkal NP (Morocco)
148 Niokolo Koba NP (Senegal)
149 Boucle de Baoulé NP (Mali)
150 Nimba Mts NC (Guinea)
151 Mole GR (Ghana)
152 W-du-Niger NP (Upper Volta, Niger, and Dahomey)
153 Waza NP (Cameroon)
154 Benoué GR (Cameroon)
155 Faro GR (Cameroon)
156 Boubandjidah GR (Cameroon)
157 Manda GR (Chad)
158 Bamingui-Bangoran NP (CAR)
159 Nana-Barya GR (CAR)
160 Zemango GR (CAR)
161 Odzala NP (Congo)
162 Mont Fouari NP (Congo)
163 Albert NP (Zaire)

Sudan
164 Dinder NP
165 Nimule NP
Ethiopia
166 Simien Mts NP
167 Menagasha NP
168 Awash NP

Uganda
169 Kidepo NP
170 Kabelega Falls NP
171 Ruwenzori NP
172 Kigezi Gorilla Sa
Kenya
173 Marsabit NR
174 Tsavo NP
175 Amboseli NP
176 Nairobi NP
177 Lake Nakuru NP
178 Masai Mara GR
Tanzania
179 Serengeti NP
180 Arusha NP
181 Ngurdoto Crater NP
182 Selous CA
183 Gombe Stream GR
Malawi
184 Nyika NP
185 Kasungu NP
186 Lengwe NP

Mozambique
187 Gorongoza NP
Zambia
188 Sumbu GR
189 Luangwa Valley NP
190 Kasanka GR
191 Kafue NP
Rhodesia
192 Mana Pools GR
193 Chewore GR
194 Inyanga NP
195 McIlwaine NP
196 Ngezi NP
197 Matopos NP
198 Wankie NP
199 Victoria Falls NP

South Africa
200 Kruger NP
201 Mkuze GR
202 Hluhluwe GR
203 Umfolozi GR
204 St Lucia BSa
205 Natal NP
206 Loteni NP
207 Willem Pretorius GR
208 Mountain Zebra NP
209 Addo Elephant P
210 Bontebok NP
211 Kalahari NP
South West Africa
212 Etosha Pan Sa

Index

Page numbers in *italics* refer to illustrations or captions to illustrations.

Picture Credits

Key to position of picture on page: (B) bottom, (C) center, (L) left, (R) right, (T) top; hence (BR) bottom right, (CL) center left, etc.